# MIND WARDER

## HOW A SHIFT IN PERSPECTIVE CAN POSITIVELY TRANSFORM YOUR LIFE.

For a life worth living...

Alina Balmos :-x


**by**

**Alina Balmos**

ISBN: 978-1-5272-1094-3 (sc)

ISBN: 978-1-9998-3361-9 (e)

For more information, please visit www.alinabalmos.com

Instagram: alinabalmos_awosl



Alina Balmos rev.date: 6/19/2018

# CONTENTS

# Dedication

For the wonderful gifts of life and love,

I dedicate this book to my loving parents Radu Balmos and Anca-Simona Balmos, who are and will forever be my greatest heroes and teachers.

To my wonderful brothers Radu-Andrei Balmos and Sanda –Gabriela Balmos who believed in me and supported me in fulfilling my dreams.

To my dearest brother, Paul Balmos, my dearest nephew Raul Trombitas, and also to Lepsa Geanina, who is a great friend and second mother to me, as well as a wonderful caring wife to my father. My love for them kept me strong during my hardest moments in life. I owe everything I am TODAY to them. I love you all from the bottom of my heart!

Special thank you to all my family members whose names were not mentioned, and to friends for existing and being part of my life.

To Ana Natalia Vasarhelyi, thank you for being my little sister and for supporting me every day. Special thank you to my best friend Alexandrina Pop Valeria, who took care of me and supported me in my hardest times!!

I also dedicate this book to all staff members from HOSFORD HOSTEL. Through their unlimited support and care, they changed my view about life, people, and helped me discover my life purpose. Without them, this book would have never existed.

Thank you to everyone that crossed my path and inspired me to write this book!!

With love and appreciation,
Alina :X

# Introduction

As I tried to understand what happened in my life and how I could make such an extraordinary change in my personality, I found my passion in discovering how the mind works.

Throughout my life, I've studied the attitudes and behaviours of people. I've listened, watched, studied, and analyzed both those who are successful and unsuccessful. I wanted to know the difference. I wanted to know how I could feel such a strong pain inside of myself when I was too young to even know what life was all about. I wanted to know how I could change from being very slow in accomplishing tasks to being very fast and active; or transform from having extremely poor self-esteem into being a very confident young lady. How could I change from being a child that everyone thought was a dummy, who wouldn't be able to accomplish much in life, and transform into a strong, independent woman?

All I could hear around me was "People don't change! This is who I am and I can't change!" and even, "You can't change!" None of this made any sense for me because I experienced change; so, I didn't understand what people were trying to say.

From a very young age, I had questions about life such as, "Who am I?", "What's my purpose?", "Who decides where we are born?", and "Is GOD actually real?" I questioned life in every way possible! My most frequent questions were, "Why me? What did I do to deserve this painful life?", and "Why does everything seem to always work against me?"

Have you ever found yourself asking those questions?

You may not have asked the same exact questions that I have asked, but I'm pretty sure that you have had some similar inquiries. At some point in life, we all wonder about these types of things, and we should be courageous enough to ask deep, introspective questions such as "Who am I?" and "What's my purpose?" Throughout my life, I found the answer to some of these questions, and I'm going to share them with you throughout this book.

We all have a story to tell and many people have had a tough life, but I believe my story could touch someone else that was or is in a situation similar to mine and change their life in the way I changed mine.

I wrote this book to inspire and to empower as many people as possible. My philosophy can be understood by anyone, from young children to adults. This journey began with me wanting to have a better understanding about my own powers and abilities that helped me heal my internal pain. The result was so powerful and life changing for me that I decided to share it with the world, hoping it will have the same effect for you.

My mission in writing this book is to help you understand life, and discover who you are and what kind of power lives within you… to help you open your eyes to a new perspective of life and assist you in understanding the importance of your thoughts and the power of positive affirmations.

The purpose of this book is to help you connect with God, teach you how to eliminate the victim mentality, and heal your emotional and internal pain, hopefully making your journey through life easier, happier, and more fulfilling.

## WHAT IS A "MIND WARDER?

Well, when I made the decision to write this book, I had to first find a title for it. The title had to reflect the essence of the book in just few words, which was tricky. How do I describe a whole book in just few words? I started writing the most important lessons I learned throughout my life. Then, I tried to extract the most important thing from the lessons, but nothing that popped up in my mind seemed to be good enough.

One day as I was looking at the tattoo on my right hand, which says, "As you think so you become," I began to reflect on my life and make a connection between the quote and the mind warder. I remembered Jim Rohn saying, "Stay a guard at the door of your mind." Back then, trying to understand the sentence, I imagined a guardian- a protector, a warden of the mind. Then I started to read about it, and I discovered that a warder was used by kings or commanders in chiefs to signal orders; it also was described as a watcher of a gate or a tower. A prison warden is a person in charge of the prisoners in a jail.

Therefore, Mind Warder is your inner wisdom is a symbol that represents all your powers and your abilities, it is a tool if you like or a technique you can use to change your beliefs and your perspectives. I am pretty sure you know that your beliefs and your genetics are influencing your actions and your results. There's a well-known adage that perception is reality. How we see something becomes our truth which can sometimes be life-limiting and cause a lot of suffering. Every day in both professional and personal lives we face challenges, decisions and situations that cause our stress level to escalate. The ability to step back and take a different view is a crucial skill for our time.

The Mind Warder is in all humans, and with no exception. It is the ability we all must develop in order to create the life we desire. We have the power to change and decide what we allow in our lives and our minds. You just need to acknowledge it.

On the following pages, I'm going to share with you a picture of my own Mind Warder the way I see it in my own mind. It is an extremely powerful method I use to get in control and fully understand the true power that resides within.

I STRONGLY RECOMMEND THAT YOU CREATE YOUR OWN MIND WARDER! GET A CLEAR PICTURE OF IT AND PRINT IT IN YOUR MIND!

After you imagine and create your own Mind Warder, pour into it the following abilities: The ability to be the observer of your mind

The ability to be the protector of your mind

The ability to create your own reality

The ability to change your beliefs

The ability to heal.

Pour all these abilities and power into your own Mind Warder. After that, put him in charge, and order him to guard your mind and trust in his abilities. This is a truly powerful method to acknowledge your power and use it!!

I imagine the Mind Warder as a strong man, a powerful warrior, a protector, a warden. The way I use it works extremely well for me, and I'm also going to share my method with you. You can use my method, or you can find your own way of doing it. The purpose of it is to get in control!

I see myself as being the Queen/King/The Boss, or whatever you want to call it. I am the one in charge, the one that controls and gives orders; and the Mind Warder is my protector, my servant, and my guardian. Therefore, he obeys my orders and protects me, and I call in to his power when I need it. After using it for so long, I am now to the point where I don't need to call in his power so often; my mind is much more calm, relaxed, and more in control than it used to be. What I 'm now doing is paying attention to the thoughts that come and go through my mind, and analyze how I feel and why I feel that way. When I have negative thoughts or musings that do not do me any good, I immediately change those perceptions to positive ones. That's the Mind Warder- the ability to watch everything that's going on in your mind and be in control at the same time. In that way, the outside world doesn't have the same power over my way of being or feeling anymore. Using the Mind Warder, I managed to break the cycle of negativity in my life and free myself from the victim mentality.

Imagine if you can that your mind is like a garden, and your positive thoughts are like the seeds-you need to plant them every year and take good care of them. The negative thoughts are like weeds- they grow fast everywhere, all the time. If you want to have a productive garden you need to take care of it, clear the weeds repeatedly, and water the seeds. It requires hard work, daily work, and sweat; sometimes, bad weather is going to come, and you will struggle saving the plants. There could be too much rain, or no rain at all; or there could be bugs invading the garden, but whatever you plant and take care of is going to grow eventually. For example, if you want to have a happy, peaceful, abundant life, you must plant only happy, positive, seeds (thoughts) in the garden of your mind. Within your positive thoughts is the connection with the source of energy and well-being. It is your connection with God. If you don't plant anything, or if you ignore the garden, you waste a good land that was created with a high purpose.

The type of seeds that I plant will eventually appear in my life. If I do not take care of my garden, the weeds will take over my garden. From the moment that I understood this concept, I became very careful with what type of seeds I plant in my own garden.

I replaced the TV with books, and exchanged movies for personal development seminars, audio and video courses, and life experiences. I carefully choose what type of music I listen to and with whom and in what way I spend my time. This is what made all the difference in my life.

## MY PERSONAL MIND WARDER

I am going to take you on a journey through my life! Are you ready?

Get yourself comfortable! Right before we begin, I want to wish you good luck in finding whatever are you looking for, and I hope you will take with you the most important lessons life offered me through this journey!

It is also important to mention that all the book content is based on personal experiences, lessons, and personal methods I used to face struggles, depression, and to find and connect to my own power. This book expresses my own personal philosophy after 3 years of daily studies and research. The terms I use to describe these abilities are not the real names; they are names I created for myself to have a better understanding on how our mind is working. With that said, let the journey begin!!!

# CHAPTER 1

# Life is a One-Way Trip. It Is A Beautiful Journey Into the Discovery of Your True Self.

*"Life is not what you get, it is what you become in the process."*
— Alina Balmos

Life shapes us in many ways throughout our lives, sometimes in good ways and sometimes bad. I now understand that the way in which we live life is our choice and how we shape our personality and our thinking is our responsibility. Back in 2013-2014, all I knew about life was that it was hard. I felt a continuous struggle for survival, and I was not ok with that. There were wealthy people in the world, and the way in which they lived their wonderful, extravagant lives made me realize that life is about more than toiling; and I wanted to know what it was like to experience that!

I felt that life had something personal against me when all doors of opportunity closed in my face, but I decided to fight back. I began to force my chances by kicking down the padlocked doors; and I pranced inside of the unfamiliar, full of hope and confidence for a better life. However, I walked into something that became my true hell, and my worst nightmare.

In 2013, I worked as a waitress in a restaurant and I gave my best effort. I worked tirelessly, and I never said no. I washed dishes, cleaned toilets and washed floors, but my efforts were never appreciated. After one year, I asked to be promoted but they refused, and in a weak moment of anger and being emotionally fragile after just breaking up with my boyfriend, I resigned from my job with only two weeks left to find a new job.

My mother depended on me, and I had just brought my brother to live with me to help him find a job. What mistake did I make?

There was no way to get rehired at the job that I'd quit. Who was going to pay the rent and support my brother and my mother? I was desperately looking for a job- any kind of job! But my search yielded nothing. I was desperate, wandering the streets, and didn't have the courage to tell anyone what I had just done.

Time was passing. There were only three days remaining until my last day of work at the restaurant, and still I had found nothing to replace the job that I had just quit.

One evening I decided to walk home, and a girl handed me a flier. Usually I wouldn't bother looking at them, but I did look on this one.

It was a blue flier, and on it was written with big letters 'Girls needed urgently! No experience required, immediate start!!!'

I arrived home and I called immediately. There was a very nice lady who answered, and she promptly organized an appointment to explain the requirements for the job.

I went to the interview, and the lady explained to me what I had to do. She said that all I had to do was sit in a front of the camera, do what I wanted, and talk with random people from all over the world. She asked me to give it a go for a few days. I couldn't see any other option at that time, so I decided to give it a try.

She placed me in a small room on a comfortable couch in front of the computer. Everyone started to say, "Hello! Welcome!" I started to receive compliments and hear nice things about me from some people I never knew or met in my life. I felt accepted, respected, and seen by others for who I truly was. Honestly, I received more respect from the people from the computer than I ever really had in my entire life.

But from day one on that job, I started living a lie. I had a different name, I "lived" in a different country, and my everyday life was a lie- I was a fake.

I was good at online phone chatting, where I simply listened to people's problems. I was too shy to do anything else. However, video chat, which required virtual sex with strangers, was not something that I could bring myself to do. Three days later, I decided that the job was not for me, but the owner of the business "saw something" in me- which was never there from the beginning- and he offered me a deal.

He offered me a good monthly salary for six months, just to come in and put on my best performance in the front of the camera. There were no requirements on how to be or what to do. I didn't want to do it, but I didn't have any other option at that time. I had to either I accept the job and deal with my emotions, or end up on the street with my mother and my brother. It was one of the hardest decisions I ever made in my life. Saying 'yes' was like selling my soul just to survive for a better life for my family and for myself. I didn't want to "just survive" anymore. I wanted to live! So, I said yes and accepted the job. I wanted to end the cycle of poverty in my family and in my life. The desire for wealth and the need to survive blinded me and led me on a path of self-destruction. It was a path littered with drugs, dirty money, sex, lies, and misery. I walked on that path for a very short while- just enough to see how it looks and where it leads.

I felt miserable. Being a virtual call girl was the hardest thing I ever did in my entire life. Every day, I talked with people, telling them lies to lure them into a private session with me (a private session was the only way you could make money). In these sessions, I would do whatever they asked me to do (get naked, dance, or just simply talk as friends, etc.). I was hurting so much inside and I felt so insignificant. Many nights I cried, and months were passing, yet I couldn't make any money because I didn't offer anything other than my presence in front of the camera. I felt useless.

I couldn't find a normal job. Every day I was telling lies about who I was, and before I even knew it, I began to live my lies. I started to create my own world there in the front of the computer.

I was surrounded by nice people with good hearts, but they were lonely people who lost themselves in reality. I met all kinds of people- rich men who were miserable and lonely, faithful husbands that lacked love and attention from their wives, and people with all kinds of issues. I met wives that needed some attention and needed a woman to talk with. I began to spend day and night there, and I became addicted to the fake life. I never actually made any money being naked. The most money I made was by listening to the problems of other people. There were some that paid me to listen to my problems. Others paid me just to offend and humiliate them. They were paying me to insult them, call them names, and hurt them in the worst possible way. I was not very good at doing that but as long I was paid to do it, I gave my best. I learned so many things about life and people. I got to one point where I knew what I had to do to make money, but I couldn't do it. Financially, I was living a little better than I used to and by this stage, both my mother and my brother had started new jobs. I was buying new clothes every day because doing that made me feel happy for a short time. However, regardless of what I did, I still went to sleep hating myself. I had sleepless nights and loads of nights with tears in my eyes. My behaviour and emotions began to raise questions.

I was missing from home most of the nights and I couldn't provide the honest reason as to why. Since my mom and brother lived with me, we all shared one room. Mom and I were sleeping on an ancient, damaged bed and my brother slept on the floor. My mother and my brother found out that I was doing video chat and I was embarrassed. I was ashamed of who I was.

The 9 months that I worked that job felt like pure torture. During that time, I met a man from the United Kingdom online. He seemed to be a nice old man who was suffering from loneliness and had no true purpose in life. He tried to convince me to move to the UK, promising me that he will help me to create a better life for myself and my family, get a job, and be independent. He said he was rich and he would offer me a place to stay by myself, and that he would give me a job because he had loads of connections. He went on to share that he lost his children, his purpose, was lonely, and he wanted to feel useful for someone.

I was young, very naïve, and I believed him! I was desperate to get out of that life of lies. Although my job was only place I felt accepted, I was only accepted for who I was pretending to be. I began to fear my reality, and I was afraid of what people around me would say about me or how the rest of my family would react to what I was doing. I was surrounded by lies everywhere I turned. I knew I had to get out of that situation before it was too late. I could see that I was walking on a path of destruction. My brain was like a broken record, and my mind could only focus on one sentence - " I'm going to change my life and I am going to break the chain that keeps my family down. I'm going to change my life and I'm going to break the chain that keeps my family down!!" Poverty had to stop with me and with my generation!

I knew I had to quickly change the direction I was heading. I knew I was more than what I'd allowed myself to become. I had envisioned myself as a prostitute, selling my body every day to be able to support myself, being dirty, and a drug addict. The thought of that type of future terrified me!

When that man offered to help, it felt like a miracle, and a chance for a normal life. Having access to an honest job and a peaceful sleep felt extremely promising. It came like salvation! I heard this quote as a child: "You can't go from poor to rich by being honest, and sometimes in life you have to make sacrifices and become friends with the devil until you cross the bridge!" Therefore, when this man showed up, I followed the advice from that quote, accepted his offer, and made the decision to move to the UK with hopes and dreams of a better life and future for myself and my family.

On my last visit home, my father sat down on the chair with a bottle of beer next to him. Gianina, his wife, made coffee for me and I took a seat at the edge of the bed. Looking around the room, nothing seemed to be different; but I was surprised when I noticed that everything I could see was made by my father's hands. The chair, the table, the oven tiles on the wall, and the walls he painted. The furniture was made and designed by him. A short while after, I noticed new toys for my brother that were made from wood. They couldn't afford to buy him new toys, so my father made him a guitar, two swords, and a little hammer. I felt so proud of my father. He did the best he could for my brother. However, my heart was overtaken by pity because they didn't deserve the life of poverty they were living!

My brother was watching cartoons on TV, and he saw a commercial with a child eating some sweets. He started to cry, and with his hand up high, begged that child to share with him.

It broke my heart. Tears were coming from my eyes and I felt powerless. We all witnessed that moment, and I looked straight to my father. How painful can that be for a parent? He let his head down, with his elbows on his legs and said nothing. My father's face was so sad. There was no twinkle in his eye and no hope for the future. His eyes were like the eyes of a prisoner awaiting a death sentence. His white hair was unkempt and dirty. His hands were so brown and full of scars from so much hard work! I was willing to do everything just to put some hope in his eyes and replace some of his pain with a little happiness; and making my father proud of me seemed the only way I could achieve that.

I couldn't stand it anymore. I was willing to do everything it took to change my family's situation. In that moment, attaining more for myself and my family was all that mattered to me.

"Dad, I have decided to go work in another country. I'm tired of this life. I'm tired of living just to survive !" My father was surprised, but felt happy for me.

"That's a great idea my dear. I have confidence in you, and that you are making the right decisions. You are a big girl now."

Looking away, he took his glass of beer and drank it and then he said, "I love you, Alina. Never forget that!"

This was the day I accepted the old man's offer. At that time, I saw money as a solution to all of my problems. In my country of Romania, if you are sick and you need a doctor, you must pay if you want to get his attention. Everything had a price, and nothing came for free. I became obsessed for money because it seemed to be the source of happiness.

I had started my journey full of hope for a new beginning. On the plane, I had a window seat and I just looked at the beautiful lights from the cities. When the plane was too high in the sky, I could see the light slowly disappear into the darkness. What was left of it was a tiny line that became smaller and smaller. I knew deep inside that when the light disappeared, a new beginning would start for me. When the light was gone, the time had moved two hours and the plane reached its destination. I immediately felt free, like I had lost the old me on the way.

On October 9, 2014, at age 22, I landed in Dublin, Ireland where a man 45 years older than me was waiting for me. He was my hope for a better life, a new job, and a new beginning. I had known from the beginning that it wouldn't be easy, but I also knew that in life you need to make sacrifices and take risks. However, in my desires for a better life, I seemed to have missed a critical factor: I had to share a one-bedroom apartment with a man I had just met. I was stuck between four walls with a man that lied about everything. He didn't want to help me get on my feet. He wanted to have an intimate relationship with me and get married. He had a sick mind and he used to change his mood from one minute to another. I was scared and I didn't know what to do. I had no money to go back or to run away, and all I wanted was an opportunity to get a job and get on my feet. I was desperate. Days were passing and I had no luck finding employment. I was scared, and I didn't know what to do. I couldn't do the things he wanted, or be the person he wanted me to be. However, I needed him because I saw him as my key to independence, and for a while, I used time as an excuse to keep him away from me, which he seemed to understand.

He would take me on romantic dinners and purchase me expensive gifts. He even wrote me romantic messages on the bathroom mirror. All of his efforts and advances made me sick to my stomach. He was hoping that I would fall in love with him over time. I had to face the reality: I was on the other side of the world, depending on a man that was mentally unstable. I was lying to my family, telling them that I worked in a hotel, and I was scared to go to the police because I was afraid they would send me home. Besides, going back home defeated was something I couldn't accept! Time seemed to be my only way out. I had to lie, pretend, and find all kinds of excuses why I didn't want to be touched or kissed. All I needed was a job, and every day, I was working to find a job.

There were moments when I couldn't do it anymore. I couldn't play the pretending game, and I felt lost in my own pain. Stress and depression had embarrassed me. I had no privacy, for he was always around. I was not allowed to go for a walk alone or anywhere else. My only time alone was when I had to shower or use the toilet. I felt suffocated and scared 24 hours a day, every day. I still had a glimmer of hope… the one person that knew what I had been through at the time, and that was my best friend, Alexandrina. She always knew how to listen without judging me. I knew I could talk to her, and I was embarrassed to talk with anyone else about my situation.

When I couldn't use time as an excuse, I started to pretend I was sick, using excuses like I didn't feel well, I was weak because of the new climate, and I would not eat. I used to wrap myself in blankets because I was scared. I was not sick, but after pretending to be sick for three weeks, I began to truly be sick and weak, and even when I wanted to eat, I couldn't. I decided to go to the doctor, and at my doctor's appointment I was hit in the head with the news that I was one month pregnant! That news made me fall to the floor and left me with no reaction. I refused to accept it, and it was too much for me to handle. It couldn't happen to me now! The doctor congratulated me and asked me if I was happy. I was confused and I shook my head both in happiness and terror! I was living a nightmare thousands of miles away from home with no money, no job, no security, and I was pregnant by a man I spent one night with before my flight to the UK.

Later that evening at the dinner table, I told him I was pregnant. Initially, he was angry, and he began walking around the house calling me names. Then suddenly, he became the nicest person. He used to change his mood a lot often. He said he would marry me and that he wanted to be the father for my child and make us a happy family. I didn't know what scared me the most during that moment: his unpredictable mood or the thought of us being a family.

Things were going from bad to worse. My life and my plans seemed to be all gone. How many mistakes and wrong decisions had I made? As I reflected on my situation, I finally understood that money is not everything. Where there is no peace, freedom, security and no love, money has no value. All the new clothes or expensive gifts couldn't give me any happiness. I didn't want all of that, and I never asked for anything. All I wanted was an opportunity to find a job. As for the expensive dinners and luxurious jewellery- to heck with that! None of those material items would help me have a peaceful sleep. I used to sleep every night wrapped in a blanket with pillows around me and with the phone in my hand because I was scared at the possibility of being touched.

In all of the situations I put myself in, I got a lesson and learned how naive and stupid I was… but I couldn't go back to look in my father's eyes and say "I'm sorry, I can't do it- life is too hard! I failed and you were right!" Despite my mistakes, I refused to accept that my life was finished! I refused to give up, and going back home totally defeated was not an existing option.

I remember saying to myself that the only way I would go back home defeated was dead in my coffin. I became obsessed, and my only options were either to die or get out of my situation.

In that moment was when I finally understood that when you can go to sleep with peace in your heart is when you can call yourself rich!

We used to fight every day because I wouldn't have sex with him. Four months passed and time didn't work as an excuse anymore. He would take my documents and my phone, then throw me out of the house so I wouldn't be able to go too far away. Then, he followed me everywhere I would go. I packed and unpacked my bags every week. Sometimes, when I would become really scared, he would take my phone so I couldn't call anyone. There were other days when he became violent just because I refused to be intimate, and so I had to defend myself. I was young, but I was strong enough to stop him from physically abusing me. I used my hand and my legs and I threw them at him with everything I had. I was lucky that he was just an old man.

I had to accept that I couldn't keep the pregnancy in that condition. During that time, I was living in constant fear and with no security. I couldn't accept the idea of bringing my baby in that miserable life I lived in and expose him to the same pain I grew up with. I just couldn't see any other way around it at that time and I decided to have an abortion, but everything seemed to be coming against me. The abortion was and still is illegal in Northern Ireland. I cried day and night and felt hopeless. All I wanted was to die and get rid of the pain.

After 8 weeks, I woke up one morning with abdominal pain and heavy bleeding. I was taken to the emergency room, where I was kept for hours. Everyone, including me, thought I was having a miscarriage. When I was finally examined, the doctor informed me that my baby's heart was still beating, but probably not for long, and I was sent home to wait for my baby to die.

How can I describe that pain? To this day, I still can't describe it. I cried for four days with my arms wrapped around my belly, begging him for forgiveness. It was my fault, and I put myself in that situation. For days, I had no food or water. The reality of losing my unborn child made me feel lost and ready to die with him. I hated myself, and I thought God was punishing me for wanting to get rid of the pregnancy.

On November 17, the doctor confirmed that the baby's heart had stopped, and I had no more tears to cry. I was ready to give up with life- I didn't eat, I didn't drink, and I couldn't even open my mouth to speak anymore. I felt as if my reason to live was gone. I couldn't see a way out of the misery and I felt as if I had lost everything. I was ready to let go of myself from inside. As strange as it sounds, all I felt in that moment was that if I decided to die, I could, and I was just at one decision away from experiencing that fate. Immediately, a vision of my family came to my eyes. They were looking at me with sad eyes, like I was their only hope! And then I remembered how it all began. I couldn't fail, and I couldn't give up. I had come to this country to help my family, and they needed me to be strong. They needed me to succeed so they could believe that it was possible for them also.

After that, every night I would imagine how I succeeded in helping my family. That thought was the only thing that made me smile. That feeling of pride and accomplishment gave me strength to move forward.

I couldn't eliminate my pregnancy because my body was too weak, so I had to have surgery. While I was sitting on the hospital bed receiving perfusions (a slow continuous drop by drop of blood or a drug substance in to the vein for therapeutic purposes) and listening to the drops of rain pounding on my window, I wrote this:

"Funny how life changes you- how it affects you emotionally and physically in such a powerful way. Today I'm no longer the person I was yesterday, and yesterday I was no longer the person I was the day before. The day before yesterday I was a poor, naive girl willing to do everything for a better life. Yesterday I became a selfish girl, obsessed by money and ready to sell my soul and my happiness for money and wealth. Today, today I'm willing to give all of that away. I'm ready to work hard with sweat to make my dreams come true. Today I want to be ME- the girl that makes the right decisions, the girl that is honest with herself and others. I walked on the wrong road in life. Whether you accept it or not, on the road of life you cannot go back. You can't turn around and find the right way. There's no way back, and the only direction is forward!!

Remember that life always gives you a way out. Small, narrow paths are hardly noticed by greedy eyes.

I see clearly now!"

Soon after I left the hospital, I freed myself and chose to tell the old man the truth. I said to him, "Thank you for taking care of me when I was sick. Thank you for providing food for me, and for having patience with me all this time. I truly appreciate you for all of that and I could never repay you for your kind gesture. I can be a friend when in need, I can be a daughter that you never had and help you and take care of you when you need help, but I can't be more than that to you. I just do not want to live a lie anymore. I'm sorry."

He refused to listen. He acted like he didn't hear a thing of what I said to him.

"You are just upset and you've been through a lot these days. Let's go home and get some rest. You will be fine tomorrow!" He needed me. I gave him a reason to live, and my problems kept him busy and gave him a sense of importance- that's all it was. Loneliness killed him every day. Even having me there and fighting with one other was something because it meant he was not alone anymore. He was using me. He liked for me to have problems. I later discovered that he made sure I wouldn't find a job (by doing things like disconnecting the internet) because he was afraid I wouldn't need him anymore. That's why I was still there, even though he never touched me.

When I went to pack my bags, he begged me to stay there as friends. He would help me find a job, and then I could pay him rent. I couldn't see any other alternative because I didn't know anyone and I had no money and nowhere to go. I knew that my chances to find a job would decrease if I lived on the streets while carrying all my bags with me and having no money. As a result, I accepted his offer with the condition that we were going to be separate with everything.

I told him that I did not need any money or food, and I just needed the couch to sleep on. He agreed. The next day I, found a job through an agency, which was a temporary position in a warehouse. I accepted the offer immediately. The job required manual work and the schedule allowed me to think and reflect on my life. All I had to do was wrap and make gift baskets. I worked like a robot for as many hours as I could, and for as many extra hours as I could convince the manager to give me. For two weeks, all I ate was the expired food I would find there like cheese, cakes, and chocolate. Even when it was time to go on break, I was not interested in a paid break; I wanted to work and do my best so I could get more hours. I worked hard seven days a week. The manager was so pleased that he said he wanted to keep me when the contract with the agency was completed.

Every time I went home, I went directly to bed, and he finally understood that there was no chance left. He was alone every day, finding no use in me anymore. When I received my salary for the first two weeks, I couldn't cash it because it was in the form of a check. To cash it, I needed proof of address or a bank account, and I lacked both. I couldn't open a bank account without an address, and I didn't have an address. I was stuck. I had the money but I had no money. A month passed and I had to pay my half of the rent. I didn't want to tell the old man that I did not have the money.

Finally, I received £1000 cash from my extra hours directly from the manager. That was the exact amount I had to pay for the rent, gas, and electric.

When I came home the following day around 8 p.m., the house was empty. The only items that were still there were my personal belongings and a letter on the living room table which said:

"You're never home. I'm dying alone, so I moved. I sold the car and took your £1000. Consider it payback for keeping you all those months. I spoke with the landlord and you need to be out of the apartment tomorrow before 7 p.m.!"

Good luck,

R

I didn't know what to do. Christmas was only a few days away and I was homeless with a check I couldn't even use. I spent all night packing and trying to figure out what I was going to do. In the morning, I went back to work, and I shared my problem with the manager. He offered to help me with a letter that would allow me to open a bank account. Later during the workday, one of my male colleagues asked me what was wrong, and why I looked stressed. I told him about my problem and he revealed that he lived alone in a 3-bedroom house, and he could help me! I was so happy and everything seemed to fall right into place. I had a job, and it was just a matter of time until I opened my bank account. To put icing on the cake, I even had a temporary place to stay. Later that night, after I moved all of my belongings to his house, we stayed up for a late-night chat and I asked him how much he wanted me to pay for the room. He said nothing. He didn't ask me nor anything -he just tried to kiss me. In that moment, I felt that the sky had collapsed on me and I felt like something squashed my heart. This couldn't be happening to me.

I said to myself, "Nothing is free in this world. I must pay the highest price. What am I going to do?"

I was hurting so badly. I said to myself, "Why!? When is this all going to be over? All I want is a secure job and a bed where I can rest." I didn't want a man supporting me. I didn't want sex or a relationship. I didn't want any lies anymore, but I felt that I lost control over my life. I was depending on someone else for a place to stay, and it hurt me so bad that every day I felt I had sold myself for a bed to sleep in and a chance to be able to help my family. Here I was, again putting everything else in front of my own feelings, and had gotten myself into a relationship. Everything I did felt like punishment. I put myself in that situation, and I tortured myself because of it. I felt like nothing- like a waste of air.

Soon after Christmas, when the contract ended, the manager told me that he couldn't keep me because it was a hard year and he couldn't afford to take more staff on.

BOOM!

Yet another hit. Life was determined to finish me.

I got the courage to ask out loud, "What else? What else life?! Come on, bring them all now. I'm open. Either you kill me or you let me be!"

I was crying, on my knees late at night on the big rocks beside the sea.

"I'm just trying to help my family, and I'm just trying to survive. I do not want anything from anyone! I only want a chance to stand on my own!!!" I yelled out into the darkness.

I started to go look for another job, when I received an unexpected call from the old man. He apologized for leaving me behind and for taking my money. He politely asked me to meet for coffee because he wanted to return the money back to me. Somehow, I felt I owed him something, so I accepted his offer. At the coffee shop, he asked me how I was and if I was happy. I opened up to him and was honest, and he told me that he had a proposal for me that would solve all my problems.

He said, "Alina, I will be honest. I couldn't pass over the fact that we shared the house for so many months and I never got the chance to touch you. I will give you £1000 if you will spend just one hour with me."

That was the most humiliating question that I have ever been asked! All the compassion and good will I had for the poor, old man died within that second.

"How dare you!" I said. "Who do you think I am? No, you will never touch me. I'll die first before you put a finger on me!"

He did not take my no too well! He immediately changed from the nice, kind, old man with the helping offer. He said, "I know where you live. I know your sweet boyfriend's name, and I know where he works. If you do not accept, I'll go and tell him everything I know about you. I'm going to tell him you are just using him, and I will make sure you end up alone and homeless!"

Everywhere I turned, I felt stabbed. Life was cutting like a knife, and I was in shock. As I sat in the chair in that coffee shop, I felt everything spinning around me. I remember saying, "Please God, tell me I'm dreaming. I do not know what to do, and I do not know how to react." I was praying to God but I didn't even believe in Him at that time.

I was full of anger, and I couldn't control my body. I was shaking. I said to him, "Go and tell him. Tell him whatever you want, and however many lies you want about me. I do not care anymore."

After I left, I began to fall into depression once again, lying in bed with no food and crying day and night. My partner could not understand me and to make it even worse, he found out everything about my past with video chat from the old man who kept his promise on telling everything about me.

My boyfriend began to have an attitude towards me and dragged me out of bed with force, threw my things around the house, and asked me to leave at 10 p.m. that night. He said I was depressing him. I left with nothing but the clothes on my back. For four hours in the cold night, I walked by the sea. I didn't know what to do. It was freezing outside and I couldn't feel my hands or my legs. My body was weak and I had no choice but to go back. I had never returned anywhere without being asked to, yet I went back and knocked at the door slowly.

I will never forget his reply.

"You are back? Why are you back?"

I stepped in the house shaking, pale, and I collapsed and fell on the floor crying. My clothes and all of my things were thrown around the room. I started covering myself with the clothes and anything else I could find. I was so cold I couldn't even speak.

He came and took all the things I covered myself with and he asked me to leave. He screamed at me, "Alina get out of my house! I do not want you here anymore!" I was too weak to speak.

All I could say was, "Please, just tonight. Please. I'm so cold, and I don't have anywhere to go."

Nobody had ever humiliated me in that way and I felt worse than one would treat a dog from the street. I've never forgotten that feeling. Up until that point, I thought I had experienced all the pain possible in life, but I was mistaken.

I felt lower than I ever had before. He said, "Look at yourself. Look at what state you are in. You brought this upon yourself! You could not love me. You had to cry day and night not even speak to me. I don't need you anymore. Just leave, you hear me?

Just leave my house!"

He was screaming and throwing all my belongings at me, and he forced me to sleep on the cold floor. I've never felt more embarrassed, humiliated, or hurt. I didn't close one eye. All I could think about was how I suffered my entire life since I was very young. I remembered everything from since I was three or four years old, when I felt emotional pain for the first time.

I remember it like it was yesterday- I was somewhere around four years old when, during an intense argument with his sister, my father ended up hit in the head with a piece of wood and he fell unconscious on the ground. Me and my brothers could only hear screams, and we were looking through the window to see what was going on. Although it was very dark outside, we saw our father unconscious; then, we witnessed him being dragged by his legs through the house. All three of us were crying and screaming, "Daddy! Daddy!"

Seeing my father pulled up on the stairs hitting his head on every step was so marking for me.

The pain of the memory of that night followed me for many years, and it will probably stay with me until the day I die.

For my young parents, three children were not easy to support. They struggled and they worked hard, but there were still days when we had nothing to eat. My father said that the day he saw me eating dry, mouldy bread, was the day they decided to leave the town and move back to the village where my father grew up.

In my opinion, I think it was a bad decision for my parents to move back to the village. From what I can remember, the relationship between my father and his parents was not a very healthy relationship. My mother was not getting along very well with my grandparents and my father was always stuck in the middle of having to choose. He could never find the courage to speak up for my mother, so he found his courage and relief in alcohol.

He went back to his old friends, bad influences, and bad memories from his childhood, and it was eating him from inside. When drunk, he had the courage to release that anger and he would unleash his inner wrath on the people around him. Everything changed in the flip of a second, and most of the nights when my father came home drunk were sleepless nights. Me and my brothers used to stay in our room in the dark; and when the screams started to become intense, we would slowly open the door and get ready to run and help our mother. Father never hit us when he was drunk, but he used to hit my mother (I do not know his reason for doing that). Sometimes, she had to run and hide in the middle of the night in the garden or in the basement. Sometimes, we would hide with her. We were all scared, frightened, and confused, but we all loved our father and we could never get upset no matter what he did. I remember that instead of anger, I used to feel pity for my parents.

On a Saturday night when I was around 7 years old, my father was intoxicated and screams were coming from our house like thunder; you could hear the noise five houses away. That night, my father lost his mind and he destroyed the entire house. He smashed all the windows, broke all the doors, threw out all the furniture, and smashed all the glasses. His blood was everywhere. My mother and my brothers ran away, but I stayed. I couldn't let my father alone- I felt his intention!

I watched him throw gasoline outside the house, and then I followed him into the house. He had the matches ready to set the house on fire, and a big knife which he was going to use to stab into his heart and die. He used to repeat with tears in his eyes that he wanted to get rid of the pain because he couldn't stand it anymore!

He tried to get rid of me, but I refused to leave him; so, he asked me to turn around with my back to him and for a few seconds, I did what I was told. When I realized what he was doing, I turned around, shrieking- and at just the right time. He ended up stabbing his shoulder, and a friend of his appeared at the door. His friend took him away to get him to sleep.

Neither me nor my brothers never hated my father or my mother for what they did or for the pain they caused us throughout our childhood. We stood by their side and supported them through their pain. On some nights, he would talk with us for hours about life and about how hard and unfair it is. He used to repeat constantly that "Life is not a joke or a game- life is hard", "Always think twice before you make a decision", and "Never listen to your heart because your heart will make you steal, but your mind will stop you from stealing." Now that was his advice based on his experiences and beliefs about life. They were also mine for a long period of time, but they were not all healthy beliefs, and some of his advice I misunderstood for a long time.

Sometimes when the nights became too painful, I felt desperate. When I couldn't stand my father's screaming, or my mother's and brothers' screams and tears, I would force myself into a very deep sleep. I could sleep in the same room with my brothers crying and my parents screaming at each other, without hearing anything. There, I had found my place of rest. It was so quiet there-there were no fights, no screams, and no pain; there was peace, and that felt so good.

The more intense the fights were, the more frightened my brothers were, the stronger the pain I felt inside me. I would always just watch all of them from the corner of the room. It is much more painful to watch the picture from the outside than to be in the picture! It felt like torture, like I was forced to witness those moments. The pain I felt was unbearable and I used to panic because I didn't know what to do. There was nowhere to go and nowhere to hide from the pain I felt! I couldn't stop the screams! I couldn't stop the pain!

As a child, I was very slow in accomplishing learning tasks. I was slow in everything. I always had to put in twice as much effort than everybody else just to stay at the same level with the rest. I seemed to have problems remembering things I said or I did. My parents couldn't rely on me to accomplish any tasks, and therefore, they didn't seem to have too many expectations from me or for my future.

I remember one day my mother sent me to the shop to buy bread. It was a beautiful summer day and I was around 7 or 8 years old. I started singing and jumping around, picking flowers on my way to the shop. As funny as it sounds, a half an hour later I was coming home, crying my eyes out because I lost the money my mother gave me for the bread- and that wasn't the first or only time that happened!!!

I was always afraid of making mistakes- so afraid that my brain would freeze, and because of that, I didn't think I could do anything right. I just couldn't remember a time when a teacher asked me a question in front of the class, and I would panic so bad that I literally couldn't process the information and drew a blank. I didn't believe in myself and honestly, I felt as if I were stupid. To make matters worse, my brother used to call me stupid often. He probably heard my parents talking about me having a slow mind, which for me meant I was a dummy- a retarded and useless girl. However, my life was worse than that. I used to believe that I was an ugly, fat, and freckled girl who was retarded, useless and no good for anything. I'm just a waste of air, and bad luck for everyone. I blamed myself for every bad thing that happened around me. Everything seemed to go wrong whenever I was around. I hated myself, and there was nothing good inside of me. I couldn't tell you one good thing about me. I had no love for myself. I didn't even know that loving yourself is right and important, but I thought that self-love and appreciation was selfish and mean!

Home was always stressful, violent, frightening, and loud. At school, I had no friends, and I was bullied, ignored, and rejected because I was poor. I was weak, slow and everyone thought I was a dummy. All I wanted was to be accepted, loved, and appreciated. I just wanted to be like everyone else, but I didn't know who I was or what I liked. From when I was about nine years old until age 12, I had suicidal thoughts. I remember I used to lie down in my bed, imagining my funeral. I would imagine myself in the coffin surrounded by my grieving family. Each time, my death had a positive impact upon my family and my parents. All I ever wanted was to bring happiness to my family and I was ready to sacrifice my own life for that.

I really believed that if I died and if I sacrificed my life, my family would realize how much pain they were causing us as well as one other, and they would be inspired to change. I imagined that they would become a happy family after my death. I got deeper and deeper in my own darkness, and I had a constant pain in my chest. The darkness and pain was burning me from the inside, and sometimes I felt it squeezing my heart, creating the sensation as if my chest was about to explode. It would even make my mouth dry, and it wouldn't go away. I used to blame myself for all the problems in my family. As a result, I thought I would do the world a favour if I just left for good.

One night, my father was drunk again. I couldn't stand the screams, and I couldn't take the pain that was literally eating me up from the inside, so I finally decided to bring an end to my misery and to my life. I went into my parents' room where they were fighting and pushing each other. I opened the locker where my mother kept all the pills and I swallowed them one by one right there next to my parents. I emptied every box I could find. Tears were falling from my eyes, as I swallowed pill after pill while looking straight at my parents. They were so focused on arguing and fighting that they had no eyes for me and hadn't even noticed me. I just ran away from the house, weeping and sobbing loudly. I hid in the back seat of our car, waiting for the ugly death to take me away from this wretched life I lived in. After 10 min or so, my face started to burn and I felt an intense warmth in my body. I went to sleep imagining how big an impact my death would have upon my family. Closing my eyes, I saw how on the next day my father would find me dead in the car, crying and screaming for me to come back. I saw my family become well, and my father stop drinking. I saw happiness spreading around the house, and I could see their smiles and hear their laughter. I fell asleep happier than I ever felt before.

Fortunately, I woke up in the middle of the night because it became too cold in the car. As soon as I realized I was still alive and that I woke up to the same screams, I felt so disappointed! "Not even death wanted me around!" I thought to myself.

Something inside of me, like a small voice, told me that it wasn't my time to die, and there was another way to get rid of the pain and help my family. I felt that there was so much more in me and I had a greater purpose and calling on my life! I have no explanation on how my body coped with all the pills that I took. I didn't understand how I survived that! I felt that God gave me another chance to live and fulfil my purpose; and I also felt special and needed. In that moment, I decided to stay strong and face any pain head on. I felt that God brought me in this world for a reason and whatever that reason was, I became determined find it! I never ever thought about suicide after that night.

I still had not dropped the idea of making a positive change in my family. At the young age of 12, I devised another foolish plan: I decided to become a very bad child, and when my father would ask me why I was doing the things I was doing and what could he do to help me change, I would ask him to stop drinking. As a young child, I didn't understand. I only knew what I could see, and from my perspective, drinking seemed to be the issue. In return for his word to stop drinking, I would become the best daughter in the world.

I did this intentionally for six months or so, and then I became a very rude, disrespectful girl, and I maintained these mannerisms for almost five years. I started drinking, smoking, and skipping classes in school. I was kicked out from the boarding school because of the absences. I used to disappear for days, getting drunk, and partying days and nights. I tortured my parents, and I caused arguments between my parents because they used to blame each other for the person I became. They tried to beat the hell out of me, talk nice, and they even threatened to put me in a correctional school. Nothing seemed to have any effect on me. However, I enjoyed my parents' attention, which I lacked and longed for, for many years.

When I was 14 years old and in my first year of high school, I didn't care about myself or my own body. I was not afraid of being hurt or in danger, so I easily got involved in dangerous situations with dangerous people, which led to me almost being raped. I ended up in the office of two men around 27 years of age. These men paid girls to have sex with them, make porn, and sexually explicit videos. I met them through someone that I thought was a friend of mine who invited me to meet her new friends. She took me to what ended up being an office room, and as soon as I stepped my foot in the office, the girl told me she would have intimate relations with a man in front of me, and the door was locked behind me.

She went with one of the men and had sex with him under the office desk. I didn't watch them engage in the act because I was too busy being scared and defensive as the other man tried to come close to me and attempt to touch me. He tried to have sex with me, but because I refused, he asked me for oral sex. Since I refused to do that too, he masturbated in front of me and put his cum all over me.

Because I refused to have sex or satisfy the sexual needs of that man, I was humiliated, verbally abused, and kept there by force for more than 10 hours. I was crying on my knees, punching the door with my fists, and begging them to let me go, but they kept making fun of me and calling me names. They offered me large amounts of money, cars, and all types of luxury items for what they referred to as a "one time opportunity job", which was to have sex in front of the camera… but I was not able to do anything. I refused their money and I refused to be touched by them. They didn't force me, but they verbally abused me and humiliated me until they got bored of doing it. I could never forget the last words of one of those guys. He said, "Now you see, you didn't want to be a nice, smart girl like your friend- and look! Now she gets what she deserves – (he gave her some money) –what are you going to do? You don't know where you are and you have no money to go home! I will be a good man and pay for a taxi for you if you promise not to talk with anyone about this night, and I promise you will never see me again." I did what I had to do. I accepted his offer. I never saw those men ever again, and I never spoke about it until now. Two months later, I was still afraid to walk on the street, because I was scared I would see those guys. I used to start shaking every night when I went to sleep because I felt scared, hurt inside, and I was ashamed of how those men treated me that night. I wrote what happened and how I felt about that in my journal, and then I buried it in my garden together with my fear and the pain it created so nobody would ever know what I went through. I was so ashamed!

After that, I didn't pass math due to the large number of absences, the lack of interest that I had in learning, and being too busy partying, drinking, spending time with dangerous gangs, robbing cars, and taking drugs. I had to be re-evaluated again in the summer, and to pass the class, I had to first pass an exam. The results of that exam would decide if I passed the class or if I had to repeat it. My parents told me that if I didn't pass the re-evaluation exam, they would not keep me in school anymore. They promised to keep me home to work in the garden and take care of the animals. Now, that scared the hell out of me because I enjoyed my freedom away from home too much and there was no way I could hear my parents fight every day for the rest of my life. I spent all summer locked in my room learning math by myself. I didn't get any tutor, and there was nobody to help me. I had to evaluate and study all the exercises from the beginning to end, and figure out how to do it all by myself.

They used to walk to my room ten times a day to see if I was learning and to remind me that the garden and the cows were waiting for me if I failed again.

When the exam day arrived, I walked in that classroom like my life depended on it. Realizing how I ended up and what type of people surrounded me made me feel so ashamed of myself. As I sat in front of the door, something happened inside of me and I felt like I was hit by a thunderbolt. I realized I was better than what I'd allowed myself to become! I didn't want to end up like the people that were in that classroom. I looked and studied each one of them, and I said to myself "I don't want to be like this. I can do better, and I want to be better!"

I took the exam, scored the highest grade I ever had in math, and I walked out through that door, a different me.

In a matter of seconds, I switched to being the opposite of who I had been for the previous five years. It all happened because I decided to change! I stopped drinking, going out, and partying. I cut all the bad influences out of my life. I felt like a new me… a new me that I hadn't met before and was anxious to start knowing.

Soon after I passed the exam, my father woke me up at night. He was very drunk. He said, "Alina, listen to me. I don't know what I did wrong or what is wrong with you, but you need to stop doing what are you doing. I told you- your life is not a joke. You must be careful. I can't stand watching you destroy your life!
Please tell me what I can do to help you!"

When I heard that question, something clicked in my head and I remembered the plan; finally, my moment had come!!

I stood up, took a deep breath and said, "Dad, if you would stop drinking, I will become the best girl in the world. I will listen and…." BAAAMM!!

He slapped me before I got the chance to finish my sentence. How could I be so selfish to take away from him the only thing that he would do for himself? All he ever bought for himself was a bottle of beer and cigarettes.

With a broken heart and tears in my eyes, I asked him if he thought what I said was wrong. He responded by hitting me again on the other side, and then I challenged him to hit me again! I was never scared of the physical pain. I knew that the bruises and the pain that came with the abuse would eventually go away, but the emotional pain that I felt would still be there. I was to the point where I wanted him to beat the pain out of me, but the pain never left me. Looking back, I know that we didn't grow up in a rich family. We could afford to only buy clothes two times in a year, and sometimes just once. Our parents tried to treat us all the same. If they couldn't buy for all three of us, they wouldn't buy at all! They gave us everything they had, never buying anything for themselves. My father was the one that always sacrificed his needs for ours. He never bought anything for himself. He used to say that our happiness was his happiness. They would buy us sneakers and clothes and he would stitch and sew his own until they were too damaged to be fixed anymore. Somehow, filling our own little buckets kept him going. Growing up, I observed my father always putting himself in last place and being content with our happiness. Due to the example that he set for me, I formed the belief that love means to always put the needs of the person you love ahead of your own needs, and to always think first of pleasing your loved ones and meeting their needs. If you always try to make others happy, you'll end up putting yourself in a negative situation, which is what I did…I tried to make others happy so I could benefit a little from their happiness to feel useful.

My need to be a people-pleaser, my lack of self-love, and the fact that I had no example of a true, healthy relationship created a recipe for relationship disaster. When I fell in love for the first time, I put all of my soul and body to my boyfriend's disposal. I first fell in love with his charming smile and I melted in his arms on our first kiss. I still remember every detail of the first day we met as if it were yesterday. I can see his attire, which included his purple t-shirt, his very light and snug tight jeans, with black-and-white checkered shoes. I was almost 18 and he was 16. We were two young children that needed love, yet lacked self-confidence. I loved him so much that I eventually gave up on myself and gave him everything I had. However, what I had to give wasn't enough, and he wanted more. He demanded all of my attention, and in order for him to feel secure, he wanted to be the only person that existed in my life. He was jealous of my love for my family and friends. In short, I began to allow him control of my life. I became the person I thought he wanted me to be. I dressed in a manner which he preferred, I spoke the words he wanted, and I stopped having friends because he never liked anyone. We used to have massive arguments if I waved to a colleague on the street or smiled and said hello, for he did not allow me to be friendly and nice. I stopped meeting my girlfriends for coffees and going out with colleagues at work because he would make my day so miserable. After 12 months in our relationship, he started to be verbally and physically abusive. I always forgave him because my mother always forgave my father, and I thought that this was how it was supposed to be in relationships… stay together through the good and bad times, no matter what. I felt I was not existing, and I failed to exist independently from him. I didn't know who I was.

I was trapped in my own nightmare. Around the same time I was going through all of this, my parents broke up and my mother finally decided to leave my father after 20 years of marriage. I was happy because I thought the problems were over and I would FINALLY have some peace. I was so wrong, because the nightmare was just about to begin.

My father was extremely affected after the break up. I remember seeing him stuff a bunch of pills in his mouth. I saw him trying to hang himself outside when my sister grabbed his legs. I heard him talking about his pain. I saw him suffering, and I cried with him. There was a time when he constantly repeated that he was going to die soon, and we needed to get used to the idea. He used to talk about what he was going to leave us after his death and how we all have a portion of the house as an inheritance. He also explained how to share the piece of land he owned. I remember the pain I felt; I used to cry like he already died. Each time he repeated this, I would experience the feeling of losing him. I would cry and beg my father, "Please don't die!" It was too painful. I felt my heart breaking into pieces.

My father was still alive, but emotionally, I felt as if he had already died. No tears or words could express the pain that I felt. I don't judge him. I know that he did the best he could, and I know that his intentions were good. If the thought of hurting us would have passed through his mind at that time, I know he would not have done it.

The divorce had a similar effect on my mother after she left. She couldn't get back on her feet and she left everything behind. All she took with her was a car which became her home for a while. Everything that could work against her at that time, did. She experienced deep depressions, and she swallowed her pain with alcohol. She also had suicidal attempts.

At that time, I was doing a post-high school course and was focused on getting myself in the position to be able to financially help my parents. Me and my siblings were now grown and living our separate lives, so my father lived alone in the village. My sister got married, and my mother was living in her car. I struggled with my own problems in my relationship. I was young and sleeping in the train station without food for days just to be able to further my education. Advisors at the college felt sorry for me, so they allowed me to stay there at the college for free until I found a job so I wouldn't have to sleep in train stations during the frigid winter. I could barely speak two words when I was finally called for an interview and my lack of confidence made it difficult for me to find a job. I remember spreading fliers in the cold winter for an hour or two for a mere three pounds (10 or 15 lei in Romanian money) in -3°C weather. Dressed in an Autumn jacket, I had only three shirts and my sneakers, which were designed for warm days because they had tiny holes in them. I wore them in the snow because that's all that I had to wear. There were days when I cried inside because the situation I was in wouldn't allow me time to cry. I had to put a smile on my face, keep going, and keep searching for work. I needed to make money to survive-not just for myself, but also for my parents.

My mother used to call me crying, saying that she didn't want to live anymore, so I had to leave school to look for her. Other times she would just cry and drink, then call me or my brothers and complain about how miserable she was and how much she desired to die. Sometimes she would disappear because she was too embarrassed to complain to us about how miserable she was.

Around the same time, my father was in the village depressed, alone, and in the same situation as my mother- drinking and planning his death. I was literally running from school to my mother, and then to my father. I had no money. I had to use the bus or train without paying, face the embarrassment and humiliation of being stopped and fined by ticket inspectors, and then travel by foot for miles to get to my parents who needed my support. I was living everyday with the fear that I might lose one of them one day and on top of that, I was being abused in my relationship. The pain and pressure that I felt in my heart and all over my body increased and was almost unbearable. When I walked on the street or sit on the bus, I used to cry as I reflected on my experiences and on my miserable life. I can honestly say that I was the most negative person I had encountered up until that point. I was concentrating 100% on the negative aspects of my life, and my mind came up with all sorts of other negative images and memories. As I travelled deeper and deeper into my pain, I re-lived it in my head repeatedly, which deeply affected me.

I was miserable every day. My energy was low, and I was constantly sick, even though the doctor considered me healthy. When I reached the age of 19, I was financially and physically exhausted. As healthy as my body may have looked, I felt like the walking dead. I felt the pain eating away at me, and I was rotting from inside out! I felt empty, full of darkness and pain, and at the same time I was pissed off with life! Every day there were problems, and every day something bad was happening. Most of the time, many challenges that I faced were created by my parents, which made me realize that I was not the actual issue. The problem was not me and was not in me; it was outside of me. However, it still hurt like it was me because I loved my family with all my heart.

When I was causing trouble in the family with my rebellious attitude, I was always doing what I wanted, never listening, always answering back disrespectfully, and saying things to my father like, "I will do whatever I want with my life. If I want to destroy it, I will destroy it, and it is nothing that you can do about it!" He kindly looked at me and he said, "When you become a parent, you will understand. You will understand what it feels like!"

As I witnessed my mother destitute and sleeping in her car, I felt like we switched roles and I became a parent for my childish parents. Through my pain and through the tears, it was almost as if I heard my father's voice saying once again, "When you become a parent you will understand. You will understand how it feels!"

I finally understood what he meant. I realized how it is devastating for a parent to see his children ruin their lives and see them struggle with addictions to alcohol and drugs. It is indeed the most painful experience a human can or will experience in this life. It is the most terrifying, constant, internal torture. And it is no different for a child to see her parents that way. I couldn't do anything, and my inability to help killed me emotionally… and it felt like hell. I finally understood Daddy!

I learned many lessons from my mother; yet, most of them were about what not to do. However, I'm so grateful for her because of that. She survived 48 years of poverty, depression, hard times, disappointment after disappointment, and failure after failure. She is still standing, trying every day to get better, and she is improving every day.

I never lost faith in my parents. I saw my mother happy, healthy, and independent long before she even started to change. During that time, she drank and caused problems, and no matter how many times I rescued her from abusive relationships, poverty, and even helped her get a job and start a new beginning- she went back to her struggles. However, I still believed in her, even when all my family told me to let her go because she would never change and she will drag me down with her. Regardless of this, I never lost faith in her. My mother is a super woman! My super woman.

I had faith in my parents, but not in myself. How could I lose faith in me now? There were so few happy moments that I can hardly remember them. One Sunday night, we were all sitting and watching T.V. We had only two channels: TVR1 and TVR2. A comedy show on TVR1 was called Apartment 9 and featured the characters Raba and Rosy. I was sitting on a chair next to the bed where my parents were laying, and my brother and sister were squeezed around the T.V. Everyone was laughing with tears, but I was not paying attention to the T.V. I was admiring the happiness that flowed around me. It was such a wonderful feeling, a feeling I had never experienced before!

Seeing my father with tears in his eyes, grabbing his belly and kicking the bed with his fist from laughing got my attention- I had never seen my father laughing with tears in his eyes before, looking so happy. It was so beautiful to watch, and it brought happy tears to my own eyes. That was the first day and last day I saw the happy tears of my father and that kind of happiness flowing in our home.

I always admired my parents' strength and courage. As hard and painful my father's life seemed to be, he found the courage to keep on going, and to keep fighting. For him, it was an everyday battle between his desire to end his suffering and our need of him. His love for his family won the battle over death. My parents are my super heroes!

There were no days off for my father. If he was sick, he would get up and go to work; and if he was tired, he wouldn't stop until he finished what he started. He taught me the most important principles in life- to be strong and never give up. He never talked about it, but he modelled it for us every single day and exemplified how to do it!

As I reflect to seven or eight years ago, I recall how my father broke his left ankle and had an operation. The doctor recommended him to rest and recover for six months, but after one month, my father was back to work because there were mouths to feed in the house. In deep pain, he dragged his leg after him. He used to get a full wicker basket of wood, tie it around his leg, and drag it after him into the house.

If my father could do it and if my mother could do it, if they could face all the adversity in the world and they are still standing to this day, surely I can too. Their perseverance through the toughest obstacles in life gave me motivation to push hard, even when I didn't feel like trying.

I snapped back to reality. As I slept on the cold floor that night, I made a promise to myself that I would never ever again, as long I live in this world, give someone a chance to treat me the way I was being treated. I promised myself that I would not put myself in that situation anymore! I vowed that I wouldn't ask for a dime from anyone or be in the position to depend on anyone for anything. I decided to be independent, work hard, and provide for myself and for my family in an honest way. I said to myself, "In my life, I paid for every mistake I made and for every step I took in the wrong direction. I had a painful childhood. I lived in pain and I was abused in a relationship. I lost a pregnancy. I was humiliated, lonely, homeless, and I survived suicide attempts. I paid for my mistakes, got what I deserved, and I learned my lessons!"

I got up on my feet and I said out loud for the second time, "Dear life, you've got to kill me now or let me be because I am still standing!"

I packed all my things and I left without looking back. I called a taxi and I asked to be taken to the police station.

Did I have a plan? No, I didn't. I had no clue what was going to happen or where I was heading with my life. What was crystal clear were the things that I didn't want to happen ever again in my life, and where I was not going.

I think life was finally ready to shake hands with me, and call it even because after that, my life took a whole new shape. It was as if that taxi took me to another dimension, and a new level of existence. I moved from everything happening against me to everything happening for me.

I was taken to The Hosford Hostel in Belfast by the police. I was given a wonderful, warm, and private room. They gave me food, security, and they offered me all the programs, tools, and support I needed to get back on my feet! The support workers from Hosford filled my heart with love and completely changed my perspective about life and people. Through their unlimited support, care, and dedication, I found my life's purpose, and that is to support and help others make a positive change in their lives.

Through my own life experiences, I discovered that change is possible for everyone, and it simply starts with a decision to make a change!

After two weeks, one of the support workers called me into the office and he told me that they found out that I was not entitled to any housing benefits. To receive their support, I had to qualify. The law stated that I needed at least 6 months employment in the country and since I had only been working for four months, I wasn't qualified. But they saw my will and efforts. Every morning, they observed me getting up and walking through town for hours looking for a job, despite the weather. Therefore, they decided to help me anyway, and they told me that they were not only going to support me with a place to stay and food to eat… they also offered to give me a weekly allowance of £25. I was overwhelmed. I started to cry and couldn't believe that something like that was even possible. Surely, there had to be something I had to do in return for that because I knew that nothing comes in life comes free, so I asked, "What can I do in return of your kindness? Do I need to clean? Do you need me to clean the floor? Wash dishes? What do I need to do in return?"

They answered, "Nothing Alina! All you have to do is to get on your feet, find a job, and become independent."

That moment was so powerful. I still cry every time I remember. There in that moment was when my view about life and people changed, and when I found my purpose. In that moment, I wanted to make others feel the way I felt. There is pure kindness in the world too; not just evil. There are good people in the world, and not everything is about the money. To this day, they have never asked me for anything in return.

Due to their support, I got a chance to create a new beginning in life. They gave me an opportunity and I took it with everything I had, not wasting one second.

My family knew at that point that I was not working and I was living in a hostel.

They told me so many times, "Alina, just come home. You see, there is no job there for you! Why are you staying there and struggling by yourself?"

I had to tell them that I didn't get through all of this just to go back to nothing. No, no!! I'm not going backwards, only forward. I won't give up. There was a job out there somewhere for me, and I was determined to find it. If not, I would die trying before I quit!

Members of staff from the Hosford Hostel supported me until I got a secure job and a safe place to live. It took me four months to find a job and a place to stay, and I received support all the way to the end. And they didn't even stop there! They offered me two years tenancy support which provided me with everything I needed for my new home! Hosford, for me, was a blessing from God, and a place full of angels. I owe to them everything I am today!

After I moved, I went back one day with a big box of chocolate and a thank you card. I went to say hello to the others that were there with me. Most them were still there and they had not progressed. Some of them were worse than they were prior to me leaving. I asked myself, "Why?" We all had the same opportunity and the same chance to have a new beginning. Why did so few of us use that chance, and the rest let it go to waste?

The only answer I could find was that only 20% of the people that were residents there actually saw the opportunity and took it; the other 80% never saw it as an opportunity. They didn't see the life preserver thrown at them, so they kept falling down the hole with the life preserver right in front of them. In life, there are opportunities everywhere and at every corner. You just need to open your eyes to see them!

Remember, things happen in your life and challenges will always arise. Someone said one time, "In life, you are either in a problem, just getting out from a problem, or heading towards one", but I say that it is up to you to decide in what way you let life shape you and your future.

From that moment, I left the hostel to begin a journey of independence and the progress I made was unbelievable. I began to work on myself and I had taken myself to a life coach to help me change and improve my life.

In 2015, I wrote in a small journal about the person I was. I included all my qualities and all my defects that I was aware of, and I also described the situation I lived in. I split the page in two. On the first page, I wrote who I was and on the second one I wrote who I wanted to become. In 2016, I looked back and analysed my progress and I was proud of my results.

Here are my findings:

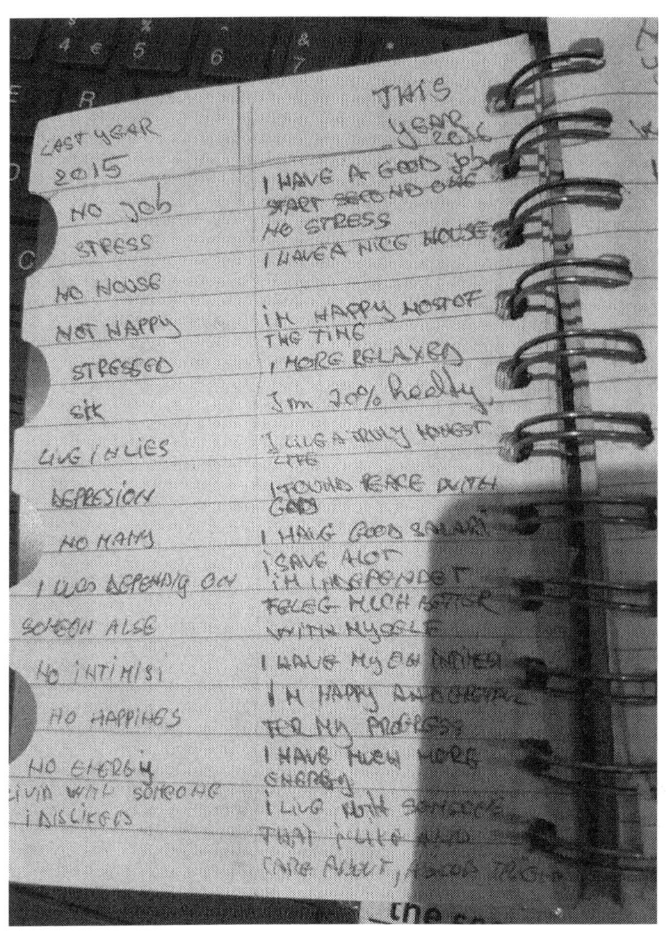
LAST YEAR
2015
NO job
STRESS
NO HOUSE
NOT HAPPY
STRESSED
sik
DEPRESION
NO MANY
I WAS DEPENDING ON
SOMEON ALSE
NO INTIMISI
NO HAPPINES
NO ENERGY
THIS
YEAR 2016
I HAVE A GOOD job
NO STRESS
I HAVE A NICE HOUSE
IM HAPPY MOST OF
THE TIME
I MORE RELAXED
I'm 70% healthy
I SAVE ALOT
I HAVE MUCH MORE
ENERGY

2015 2016

| I had no job | I have a good job, and soon I will start my second job. |
|---|---|
| I'm in constant stress | I am more relaxed |
| I am miserable | I am happy most of the time |
| I am always sick | 70% healthier |
| I am living in lies | I am living an honest life |
| I am fighting with depression | I found peace with God |
| I have no money | I earn a good monthly income |
| I am depending on someone else to survive. | I am independent |
| I have no intimacy | I'm grateful for my own intimacy and my progress. |
| I have no energy. | I have much more energy |
| I hate the person I live with | I share my house with a wonderful person. |
| I have no security | I am safe |

The change I made in the course of one year was unbelievable but somehow, I was still living in my past. I was still operating in a victim state and mentality. At the time, I had built new relationships and friendships. I had a vision for my future. I was working on loving myself, and things began to change significantly in my life, but I was still held back by my feelings for C (my first boyfriend). It had been two years since we had last seen one another, yet I still loved him. We always looked after each other in secret. As soon as we met again, we began dating again immediately and he moved with me in the U.K.; however, the relationship never seemed to work. More things seemed to show up on the reproaching list. Whatever I did during the time we were separated seemed to be a new problem. As a matter of fact, the entire past seemed to be a serious problem. He never physically hurt me again, and was never again as possessive and jealous as he was previously, but the memories of the old version of him remained in my heart and mind. I refused to accept the new and improved him. Every normal question took me back to the old days, and the same feelings and fights began again. The same happened with him- he still looked at me for who I was in the past. We were both blinded by our history, by the children we used to be, and we never really gave our new, mature, beautiful souls a chance.

As I look back now, I see two souls that resided in the past, and I realize that the powerful connection and the beyond-happiness feeling that we experienced lie in the short moments during the present. Somehow, there was always a conflicting problem, but still each time was better than the last. Each time was more respectful, more responsible, had less fights, and more peace.

We were like two broken glasses with the pieces mixed together. I was so damaged I could barely fight for myself. I was in my own battles with myself, struggling to put the pieces back together again. I just couldn't be in two battles at the same time.

I felt I couldn't operate with the external battles with him and the internal battles within myself, and it was too much for me. The relationship drove me crazy but I didn't want to give up on him. He was fighting his own battles; he felt confused, lost, and unclear on what to do with his life. Sometimes he felt stressed, depressed, and insecure of himself. I couldn't carry the responsibility of ending the relationship with the only man that I truly, dearly loved. I was weak, and I was not happy. I felt so small and insignificant in front of him. All of my attention was on his well-being and his happiness.

I totally forgot about myself and my own needs, and my self-neglect hurt so badly. I could clearly see what was happening, but I couldn't find the power to do anything. I became so far gone that I would go shopping and buy food just for him- the exact amount of food he needed for a week to keep his diet in order. I remember feeling hungry, and opened the freezer just to realize there was nothing for me. I was so angry at myself, but I blamed him. I called him selfish, and repeatedly inquired why he never thought about me I was working as hard I could at a job I hated with all my heart. He saw me crying many mornings, and I began to release my anger on him. Why was he not willing to get a job and help me out? He was just eating away at me- physically, emotionally, and financially. Once more, I ruined the foundation that I spent two years building up. I spent all my savings just to try to make him happy and to support his dream.

I really felt as if I was losing myself and destroying my life. I knew that I worked too hard and went through too much hell to continue allowing my life to crumble the way it was crumbling. One day I told him, "I love you but you have to choose. You either come with me or I leave you behind. Either way, I'm still going forward, and I refuse to go backwards any more. If that's your direction, I won't let you drag me with you."

Truthfully, I felt powerless, and my family was disappointed in me. When my father found out what I had been doing, he refused to even speak with me. I felt I was losing everything, and all I had left was my faith. I didn't know what else to do, so I began to pray. I prayed every night to my Universal God, holding Him in my arms with my eyes closed and praying in silence.

I said, "God, I place my whole life into your hands. I know there is no harm in your hands. I put my relationship in your hands God, and I believe in you! I'm hurt and I'm in pain. I'm too weak in my feelings for him. Please help us, God. If he is not the right person for me, or if we are still not ready for each other, please, please enlighten him God, because he is lost like I am. He feels what I feel. If I am so weak, give him strength to find his way, and show him his way. Give him the power to decide what's best for both of us! Please free me from being responsible for making the right decision. This responsibility has been on my back for so many years, and I can't carry it anymore."

One month later, he told me he wanted to go home because

he was not happy, and he couldn't see any future for himself in Northern Ireland. I understood and supported him in what he felt was best for him. I loved him enough to let him go and find his own happiness.

After approximately two months of depression and financial struggle, I finally got back on track, changed my job, and saved money to go and visit my family in Romania.

During my visit there, my ex looked for me, found me, and convinced me to give him one more chance to prove his love for me.

Somehow, he was more powerful than I was, and I accepted him back into my life. I used to always end up being powerless, weak, and very angry because I felt he was robbing me of everything I had, yet I didn't know how to set boundaries. I couldn't bring an end to the downward spiral and no matter how bad I wanted to, I couldn't find the inner strength to leave the relationship. I felt like I was suffocating, and I went straight back into the agony I used to live in the past. Every day I felt a life versus death battle inside of me- a joust between the love I gathered up for myself until that point, and the desire to grow and feel accomplished versus remaining in a toxic relationship because of the strong feelings I had for him.

I saw him really trying, but he was struggling to keep himself together. I had to accept that hard work scared him away. It was clear for me to see that he had a different path to follow. However, every night, I prayed the same exact prayer to God.

He became more and more confused about what he wanted. He faced depression, and I tried to open his eyes to encourage him to see the good in himself...but it was never up to me. I was facing my own battles, and I was fighting to stay strong within myself.

One month later after a massive argument, he literally tortured me mentally for four hours, and I cried for four hours straight. I thought, "I'm going to go crazy."

He constantly repeated, "Alina, when are you going to stop crying?" "Yeah, keep crying! Please don't stop! Cry!! You remember what you did, then?"

"How about when we went there and you did that. You remember?" How could you?" "Yea, keep crying. Don't stop, please!"

I thought to myself, 'Cry more? Don't stop?' I couldn't stand hearing him anymore. I covered my ears and started to sing. Making noise just so I couldn't hear him. He took my hand with force from my ears and kept torturing me with words. I locked myself in the bedroom, but he knocked the door out, and came and sat by my side. I cried and begged him to stop, but he kept on going. After four hours of mental torture, he finally broke me open. I got out of the bed, wiped my tears, and I said to myself 'That's it, enough! I'm in charge of my life. Sitting here crying, letting you torture me is a choice. I choose not to!!!' I promised myself I will never again let anyone do this to me!

There was a different power in my voice that completely changed the situation. I was no longer the victim, and he had no more power over me. He felt it, and he apologized. He asked for forgiveness. He was ignorant, and I forgave him for his lack of knowledge. However, I recognized that he put me in a situation where I either gave in or broke through, and I'm so grateful to him for that.

He told me one morning that he made the decision to leave again and go back home. That was the best for us and for him. I understood and supported him again in what he felt was best for his life, because I believed it was God's answer to my prayer. I told him there was no going back between us. I finally accepted this reality, and I felt free. He left the next day and I have never seen him face to face since then.

My opinion regarding my relationship changed throughout the years. I blamed him, and in my eyes, I was just a victim. He was the abuser, the man that wouldn't allow a smile on my face if it was not addressed to him. I blamed him for not living for so many years, and for keeping me under his control. I remember writing in detail about what he did to me, how he treated me, humiliated and hurt me in public, how he manipulated and used me, and even how he threatened to harm my family if I broke up with him.

Re-reading all the details I wrote was exactly like a horror movie.

The more I read, the more it hurt me because I finally understood. The demise of our relationship was never his fault, and he was never the reason for my pain. I caused my own pain! All the problems were coming from inside of myself, from my lack of love and feeling of not deserving any good.

Why should I condemn him and throw rocks at him now, when I was the problem all the way to the end? The problem wasn't him; it was me. I allowed him to treat me like nothing. I accepted the situation by choosing to forgive and return to the relationship. The key to freedom was always in my hands, and even when the door for escape was wide open, I refused to leave because I feared not knowing what was on the other side of that door of freedom!

I learned to never judge. He did the best that he could with the knowledge and understanding that he had at the time. To get out of the victim state, I had to change the way I viewed my entire life. It took a while for me to reach the level of understanding that I have now, and today, I can only write about how I see my life from where I'm currently standing. With a non-judgmental attitude, I take responsibility for everything I've experienced in my past.

Looking back now, I clearly see all my mistakes. Am I ashamed of who I was? Not anymore. I admit that at one point, I was extremely ashamed and I hated myself, but I also knew that I did the best I could with the knowledge I had. I valued money more than I valued myself, which brought me to the path of destruction again and again and made me torture myself. I paid for my mistakes with humiliation, unbearable pain, depression, fear, and losing my own child.

The girl I once knew died in that hospital bed on November 18, 2014 so that I could live a new life and have a new beginning!! That girl was the old me who taught me the most important lessons in life, and because of her, I am who I am today.

Forgiving others was easier for me than it was to forgive myself, but I had to let go of the hate.

I told myself, "I forgive you. Thank you. I love you, and good bye" to my former self for many days and many months. I still say 'thank you' every day to the old me for allowing me to be who I am today. I replaced the hate with love…pure love and gratitude that freed me from the past and brought me peace in my heart.

To find happiness, you've got to forgive. You've got to let go of what once was and embrace the now. Free yourself from hate and regret, allow love to heal you, and truly love yourself. Forgive yourself for whatever you have done in life. Why hate something that made you better today? You've punished yourself enough and it is time to free yourself!

In order to forgive myself and make peace with my past, I had to change my perspective about life and view it as a "one way trip". As much as we want to, we cannot go back to change the things that we have already done, or take back the words that we have spoken. We can just move on and accept things as they are or not.

After looking at life from this perspective, I made the decision to let go of the things I did not have control over and to make peace with my past so I can now live peacefully. I no longer look back with regret. I reflect on everything with gratitude. Everything

I am today is due to my struggles, my pain, and my mistakes. I no longer go to sleep ashamed of myself, and I no longer fall asleep in regret and pain. I now fall asleep with gratitude, and even sometimes with a funny smile on my face because I truly feel rich.

I'm not a millionaire. I'm just like you, but I consider myself a rich person. I have freedom, peace, and security. I have health and a family that loves and supports me. I have a warm home with a comfortable bed to sleep in. I became rich inside, and that's more than enough. No amount of money can ever buy gratitude and happiness.

Today, I see all my struggles as blessings from God that made me become the woman I am. I believe that struggles are God's wings on your back. They are wings that are meant to get you close to your dreams, to yourself, and close to God.

The way you experience life has everything to do with your perspective about life. Be open to taking risks, and don't be afraid to step forward and make decisions. You don't have to be foolish, naïve, and throw yourself into dangerous situations like I did. Choose wisely and don't fear making mistakes. Without mistakes, there are no learning lessons, and without lessons, there will be no progress. Do it wrong until you get it right. You won't lose anything, but you will learn many things.

You can only lose if you stay stuck and if you stop trying. You can only fail if you give up!

View life as if it is a journey in which all that really matters is what you become at the end of it. We go from birth to death, and that's a fact. We all know there is no way to escape from the course of life. There will always be an end to any beginning, and there will always be day after night, spring after winter, and good days after bad days. It's just the way it is and I don't think it's going to change any time soon. You may be experiencing tough times now. You may struggle or you may have been in pain for a long time and are tired. I understand you, and I know how it feels. I lived in pain and struggle for almost 20 years of my life, but I didn't give up hope and neither should you. Allow God to hold your hand and carry your pain. He will if you allow him to. Just remember that God has a purpose for all our struggles, and you have the power to get up every time you fall. We all have resilience deep inside of us but you must tap into it. You are special, and there is greatness within you! Get up, smile, and don't allow the weak moments in life to overpower you. Allow them instead to straighten you and make you wiser. Allow life to challenge you. The reward is priceless.

## CHAPTER 2

# Self –Love and Self-Acceptance: The Key To a Balanced Life

*"Love is the great miracle cure. Loving ourselves works miracles in our lives."*

— Louise Hay

Because we were poor and didn't have much, our parents always told us to share and not be selfish. They expressed the importance of thinking about our siblings and not just about our own needs. I misunderstood this concept and I formed the belief that thinking about my own needs was selfish and bad.

As a result, I ignored my own needs and never put any value on myself because I wanted to be a good person, and didn't want to be mean and selfish. I never saw myself worthy of being loved, happy with my life, or deserving of being cherished by someone. Being able to please others and get a smile on their face made me feel good, and this is what I believed that happiness was all about… bringing myself a bit of satisfaction from making someone feel good and happy. That was my happiness.

The weirdest thing is that in 21 years, it never crossed my mind that I should love myself. Everything I did was always for someone else. All I was thinking about was the needs of others. I was used to the emotional pain, and internal sadness was all that I ever knew. I didn't experience happiness, so I didn't know how else to feel. I settled with the mundane routine of life because I didn't believe that I had the power to change my circumstances. Sadness and depression were normal for me and the only thing I truly wanted in life was to be liked and accepted by others, but somehow that seemed impossible to achieve.

When I was young, I used to lie down in the dry hay during the hot summers and watch the shapes of the slow-moving clouds. On the nights with a full moon, I used to sing my feelings to the moon. I remember feeling so good, singing away my pain and my struggles underneath the beautiful stars! The moon was the only one that actually listened. I always had a feeling that I did not belong to that community or to that society. I never felt at home in my own home. I couldn't find a place to fit in, and I always felt different.

When I opened my mouth to say something or ask questions when I was with my 'friends', everyone would look at me like I was weird and stupid, and sometimes they would even laugh and make jokes about me. Everyone, including my family, seemed to always misunderstand me. Because of that, I was afraid and ashamed to speak up in front of others. Until about age 9, I had no friends. The animals from our courtyard were my friends… these were the animals that never got too much attention from my family because they were not as sweet and joyful and beautiful like the rest. I saw myself in those animals. They represented exactly how I felt: ignored and lonely. I condemned and blamed myself for being different because I was always the one with "stupid" questions. I remember making a list of questions and the list was called "Questions without Answers"! It amuses me now, as I reflect on the incident. The questions were quite interesting, and they included inquiries such as "Is God actually real?", "Is the earth really round?", "Who created the law and why do we have to follow it?", "Who am I?", "What is my purpose?", and "Who decides the family and country are we born in?"

I always tried to be like everyone else. All I wanted was to be liked and accepted by the other children, receive attention, and feel important, but I couldn't do that very well either. I simply couldn't be someone I wasn't meant to be. The fact that I wasn't true to myself made me feel lost and stuck in life.

I was actually a smart girl, and it took me many years to realize that there was nothing wrong with me!

When I left my country in 2014, I felt as if I broke the chain that kept me from being who I truly was. Even as an adult, I still had my walks at night and shared my thoughts with the moon. One evening while looking at the beautiful sky on my way home from work, I said to myself, "How interesting! We all live under the same sky, but it is still so different when you look at it from a different place!"

I moved approximately 1,397.7 miles away from everything familiar, and I was alone and without companionship. Despite everything that happened, I felt at home although I didn't have a home. I felt accepted, understood, and supported. I sensed that I belonged there. I was free and happy even when I had no job or income. I walked on the streets of Belfast with a big smile on my face, holding my head high, looking and applying for jobs like I was somebody!

I thought I was nobody, but when I walked like I was somebody, I began to realize that I was magical from the day I was born… but I was never taught how to love myself. I was not just somebody, I was ME. The SPECIAL me in the same way that you are YOU, the special you. There is nobody else like me and you because we are all unique.

If you feel stuck and can't find your place no matter how hard you try…if you feel like nobody understands you and you are constantly rejected and beaten down to the ground, that's a clear sign that you need to make some changes in your life ! There are situations where the only thing that keeps you stuck and stops you from growing is the place you live and the people that surround you. You need to experience life and you have got to move so you can see the sky from a different place.

When I moved to the United Kingdom, I had no friends or anyone to call when I felt in need. There was no one to shed a tear or celebrate an achievement with. Sometimes when I was rejected, I felt really hurt, hopeless, and was desperate to speak with someone. I was scrolling through my phone for someone to talk to, checking my Facebook list, and still couldn't find anyone. I had to rely on myself.

This made me reflect and reminisce on my previous experiences, like when I turned my back on my entire family and slept in the train station. When I was sleeping in the train station, I realized that nobody gave two dimes about who I was and what I did, so why shouldn't I take a chance on being me?

In most occasions, we are not living up to our full potential because we are afraid that we will be judged, that we are going to lose our friends, or we won't be popular anymore and may end up being alone. Then, we try all of our lives to be like everyone else. We wear clothes that are trendy instead of the clothes that we love wearing, and we allow our income levels and occupations to define us. We think we are what others are saying about us, and we equate our identity with the things we possess. When we lose all that we have (even when we have nothing), we lose ourselves too; and then we become weak and powerless.

I agree that being alone is scary, painful, and the mere thought of loneliness frightens you, but sometimes you must have the courage to be yourself even when people will judge you, and even when you feel lonely from being rejected by friends and family.

You need to find the strength to go through the pain. If you can do that and persevere until the storm ends, everything in your life will change! You will eventually attract the right people who dress like you, share the same beliefs, and who have the same goals and aspirations. Soon, you will be surrounded by friends and people that will support you and encourage you to be yourself.

You need to be willing to go through the pain, overcome the fear of being alone, and you need to stay committed to your true self all the way. If you want to attract the life you desire, you need to love yourself unconditionally and in the same manner that a mother loves her child. I failed to love myself and by doing that, I was creating damage in my life by ignoring my wants, my destiny, and my needs. I never dared to ask what I truly desired, what I needed, and what would make me happy because I didn't feel worthy of accepting anything good coming my way. I hated my appearance. I was too short and fat, my hands were too big, my hair was not nice, and I thought that God created me by mistake!

I was 22 years old when I first heard the idea that I should love myself. I decided to ask for help and hired a life coach. I felt as if there was something I needed to do but I couldn't figure out what it was. In one of the sessions, Jenny, my life coach at that time, talked with me about this idea that I should love myself. My first thought was "She is talking trash because she tells me to be selfish!" In the beginning, I couldn't accept what she was telling me because I doubted it! However, I was willing to try anything that could help me to get better. I was willing to understand this concept of loving myself which she was sharing with me. In the back of my mind, I told myself that if what she was sharing with me was true, from a scale of 1 to 100, the possibility for me to change my life was 1%, and that meant that 1 % was an opportunity that I needed to take. So, I took advantage of the opportunity.

Using my coach's belief about self-love was one of the best decisions I ever made. I listened to what she said and it made sense!

How can you expect to be loved and respected if you do not love and respect yourself?

I was thinking, "My God, I do not know any person with confidence who loved, respected themselves, and who would put themselves in the same situations which I allowed into my life". As a result, I accepted her belief about self-love until I found strength to believe it for myself.

I read a nice quote somewhere which states, "To believe that your self-worth is dependent on the shape of your body is your version of believing that you are a purple pig".

It is that crazy!

Your body is just the costume of your soul. It is the vehicle which houses your soul. Your body is the only thing you have to carry you throughout life, and regardless of the shape or colour of your body, you should be grateful for having it. Value it and take care of it like it will be the most valuable thing you possess, because it is!

Your body allows you to experience life, feel joy, accomplish goals, fulfil missions, and live. I believe that as souls, we are all equal and we all have the right to exist in this world to experience life and be happy. We were all born to be great and we all have greatness within ourselves. We are all miracles of God!

If you still believe that you are not good enough, ask yourself, "I'm not good enough compared to whom?" We are all different. We are all miracles of God and miracles of the universe. We are all equally deserving, equally strong, equally powerful, and unique. Your uniqueness is your gold mine!

Who says you are not good enough? To whose standards are you being measured? Life is all about the process and the journey. It doesn't matter how fast or slow you go, how fat or skinny you are, your ethnicity, or your size. There is no gold medal in life, nor is there a first place. Everyone has his own path to follow his own obstacles to overtake and his own lessons to learn. All that matters is that you achieve the thing you truly desire, which is to step on the top of your own mountain to reach your own successes by simply being the best you that you can be.

You will never feel truly accomplished as long you are trying to be anything else than what you are already created to be. You can only feel truly accomplished and successful by stepping on your own mountaintop! You can only do that by being you, for exactly who you are. The world needs you, and believe me, there is nothing more liberating than allowing yourself to just "be", knowing you are enough.

Slowly, this idea of self-love and self-respect was sticking to me, and for more than one year, I used affirmations every morning to help me change the way I saw myself. I used to play audio self-love and self-respect affirmations when I was cooking and eating my breakfast. What I actually did was create a shift in my thinking by reprogramming my mind with positive love affirmations. I did this routine every morning, no exception. To be honest, I still keep the tradition even until this day. For me, affirmations are like vegetable seeds which I plant in the garden of my mind. If I want ripe tomatoes, then I plant tomato seeds. If I want be prosperous, then I plant prosper seeds. If I want to love myself, then I plant self-love seeds and so on.

For any change you desire to make, the only thing that actually needs changing are your thoughts. Your love, your acceptance, and your confidence comes from your thoughts. For example, if you want to improve your confidence, all you have to do is to change your thoughts by using affirmations that will help you grow your confidence.

Every morning, as soon as you wake up and before you even check your phone, make sure you read, listen, or silently repeat the following affirmations:

I deserve the best, and I'm beautiful in all ways.

I respect who I am.

I'm confident in all aspects of myself.

I am powerful

I'm confident with who I am.

I release negativity.

I'm healthy and happy.

I love me just the way I am.

I like the person I 'm becoming.

I deserve the best.

I have an attractive mind, body, and spirit.

I love myself exactly for who I am!

I am deserving of all goodness, and all greatness.

I am unique. I am special. I am a miracle. I respect and truly love myself for that.

I am important. I value myself. I truly love myself.

I truly love my life and am grateful for everything that I have!

I deserve to be happy, loved, and to live in abundance!

If you go to Youtube.com and type in the phrase "Self-love Affirmations", you can listen to some powerful affirmations and statements. Believe me, it works. If you are patient and consistent, you will see changes in the way you see yourself, how people see you, and how they treat you!

I also created a painting with a beautiful message as a reminder saying, Alina, you are wonderful and I LOVE YOU!

This is one of the best days of your life. Everything is working out for your highest good. Everything you need to know is revealed to you and whatever you need comes to you at the right time!!

All is well,

Your true self.

I worked in a place where almost all of my colleagues disliked me. I was bullied, discriminated for being a foreigner, and humiliated every day! It was the most negative work environment I've ever experienced. The department manager seemed to be on my back every day, always complaining about me. I remember that it was hard and I struggled; sometimes, I would cry on my way home from work. However, the money was good, and my plans and dreams were bigger than the pain they caused me. I was used to that. I grew up being bullied, disliked by people, talked about behind my back, or forced to deal with people making fun of me. I used it as motivation to keep going and used the negative situation and pain in my favour.

I used to listen to the self-love and self-respect affirmations for 30 minutes each day. Every day before work, I would meditate and energetically send love to my work place and to my manager, to the actual building, and to all my colleagues.

I do not know if my colleagues or manager ever changed,

but I surely changed! I changed the way I saw my job and myself, and I started to become more confident and stand up for myself. Keep in mind that although I was at that job 42 to 48 hours a week in that negative environment, I still made the change. After seven months, work was just a place I needed to be to get where I wanted. I used to go to work daydreaming with a big smile on my face. Then, I would work and return home with all the stress and pressure gone. I could tune out people who chose to badmouth and belittle me. I was working in my connection with the Source (or God as we call it). I left that place because the money was not good anymore, and I felt I deserved much more.

I moved to a job where I felt at home. Everyone was friendly, respected me, and appreciated my work, and I couldn't believe it! Nobody in my new job knew how I was unstable just a few months prior. They were unable to notice the different me (because they didn't know the 'old' me) - but I certainly noticed how I changed! I could see it mostly in the way that people treated me. It was amazing.

I was extremely proud of the progress that I had made. I jumped for joy on the inside because I changed my mind and the way that I felt each day.

For example, the first time I stood up for myself, I was not embarrassed of who I was or how I felt. The first time I stood up to a man was when my boundaries were not respected. I remember when I met a man at a house party through some close friends. We started to chat and spend time together. After two weeks, I found out that he was and had been engaged to lady for 10 years, and they lived together. When I confronted him, he tried to manipulate me and convince me that he really liked me. I felt like I was torn between reverting back to the old me and standing strong in my power as the new me…and this time, the new me had more power. For the first time, I had the power to say I deserve more than that and I kicked him out of my house. As I closed the door behind him, I was so happy and proud of myself that I began to jump around the house screaming, -"Yes girl, you did it!!!! " It is unbelievable how just one year ago, I had no idea what boundaries were or how to establish them. Learning about boundaries and the importance of self-love made such a huge difference in my life.

Watching and observing my own progress was and still is unbelievably beautiful!

As soon I began to love myself, everything changed around me. I turned into a different person, and I began to be positive and happy most of the time; I felt happy every day, even when I was stressed about lack of money or family problems. At the end of the day, I was still happy and grateful for the person I had become. I was the happiest I had ever been in my life. To put the icing on the cake, my family life improved also: my parents stopped drinking, I could once again see that sparkle of hope in my father's eyes, and people around me changed. I began to meet people who were more friendly, helpful, kind, and generous. It was amazing how my confidence grew and increased day by day.

Now, for the last 3 years I studied the attitudes and behaviours of people. I've listened, watched, and analysed successful and unsuccessful people, and I wanted to know the differences between them. I wanted to know what I did different than others that allowed me to make this change in myself. It is interesting what you can discover when you look at the world from a non-judgmental position by just simply observing what goes on around you.

One of the cruel truths that I came to discover is that the majority of people are not willing to do what is required to improve their lives because it is easy to do what's easy instead of doing what's best for you.

I often meet people who know exactly what they should do, how to do it, and why; however, they choose not to do it. Why? Because is so much easier not to do it. For example, it is so much easier to stay in your comfort zone, sit home and eat ice cream, watch TV and cry about the way you look than it is to get your butt out of the house and to the gym. It is so much easier to just give up and go back to what you're used to than it is to challenge, learn, and stretch yourself. It is so much easier to just go with the flow and take whatever is coming than is it to be in control of your life. It is easy to just mourn and complain every day than it is to act and solve a certain problem.

Some people will laugh and make fun of the silly things they must do to improve their life. Are you a part of the majority? Or you are part of the five percent that will do what is necessary to improve their lives? For the 5%, those necessary things are not silly things. They use techniques to improve their lives, and they are 100% committed to the process.

I know that if you are now reading this book, you are either heading towards the 5% or you are already a part of it, which is awesome! Congratulations!!!

The only time I made an important change to create progress within my life was when I was kind, compassionate, and patient with myself instead of hating myself for not getting things done. For instance, if you hate yourself and you are very hard on yourself because you haven't kept your diet today, if you feel disappointed in yourself for having that cake, and for all the mistakes you've made, stop! Please stop yourself from having these negative emotions!

Treat yourself like a little baby who learns every day. We do not blame babies for not knowing how to talk, how to walk, or make decisions, do we?

As adults we have patience with babies because we know that it takes time for babies to walk or talk; it is a process, where every step at the right time matters. Some babies need more time than others to master these skills, and no matter how long it takes, a baby never gives up on trying to learn how to walk or to speak.

Like a baby, you need your own time to learn new things to develop new habits or skills.

The next time that you fall short of accomplishing your goals, be gentle and kind to yourself. Enjoy a nice, relaxing bath, simply believe in yourself and in your abilities, and your challenges will become easier if you do not stress about them. You are still that baby with the "never give up attitude", and you can accomplish whatever you put your mind to! Just stop obsessing over the situation and trust the process. Most importantly never give up trying and be kind with yourself. Have patience, give yourself time to learn, and accept mistakes as part of the process. It is a tough mission to commit to improve yourself every day. There is a battlefield between who you are and who you want to be; however, you are the only thinker in your head and therefore, you are the big boss of your life. The final choice and decision on the path you want to take in your life is yours! Are you going to sleep in or get up when the alarm rings? Are you going to eat healthy, or are you going to eat tasty (but unhealthy) foods? Are you going to work out, or are you going to feel sorry for the way you look? Are you going to make the required effort to reach your goals or you are not going to be bothered? You need to be determined to make a positive change. You must plant the seed of the "never give up" attitude deep in the ground until it forms strong roots in your mind.

No battle lasts forever; someone will lose and someone will win. Eventually, you will develop peace within yourself. Who you give power to is your choice. You should always choose to focus on what is best for you, and no matter what, keep calm because tension blocks the flow of thought power and your brain cannot operate efficiently under stress.

Another point which I acknowledged, studied, and I analysed about people is the fact that a good majority of people like to hear what they already know because hearing something that reaffirms them and provides validation makes them feel secure, confident, and smart. On the other hand, when people hear something that will turn their life upside down, they get scared. They simply refuse to accept or acknowledge the scary information that threatens their comfort zone.

I've also met so many people who feared new opportunities and never progressed much in life. They stayed in the same job because they either did not think they could get better jobs, or they convinced themselves that they couldn't do a better job than they were doing; or maybe they stayed in the same miserable relationship just because they couldn't see their lives without it. I was one of those people! I stayed in a job that I hated with all my heart and I used to cry in the mornings when I didn't want to go, but I went anyway because I didn't think I could find a better job. I kept that job until I was eventually fired. I also stayed in a relationship that was unhealthy and physically abusive just because I did not believe I would find someone who could love and treat me better. I believe that lack of self-love is what keeps people in these situations.

Looking at it from my own experience, I had formed strong beliefs of self-hate and feeling undeserving because I believed that self-love is selfish. Beliefs created by thoughts like "I hate myself. Who am I to be important? It's selfish loving myself," etc., are beliefs which I formed that determined my day, my decisions, my ideas, and my actions. These beliefs can easily lead to:

You exercise regularly- only if you have someone to keep you accountable.

When you do not have someone to push you anymore, you feel lost and powerless, which can also lead you to...

Lack of energy-----→you do not feel comfortable with your body, and that affects your actions-----→ which stops you from having the confidence to express your own opinion and this can affect you in three ways

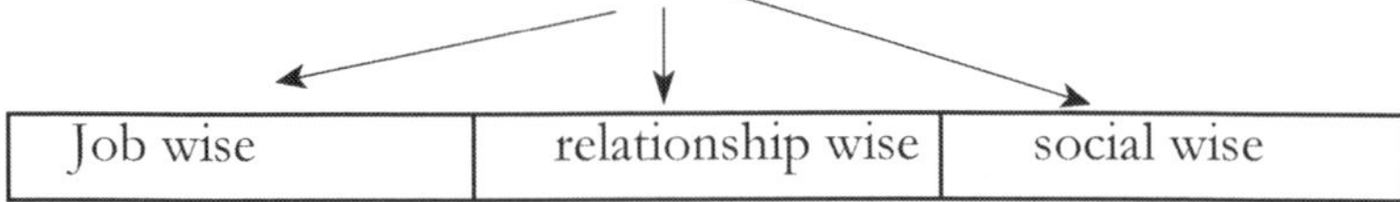

Which also makes you become a people pleaser.

You make everyone and everything more important than yourself.

Most of the time you put yourself in unpleasant situations for you, just because you do not know how to say no

You always try to make people feel good around you, just so you can feel good about yourself.

You do things that you don't feel like doing.

You always give others first the chance to choose what is best, and you always settle with what's left.

All this will eventually lead you to:

| | |
|---|---|
| 1.Keep yourself in an unhealthy relationship. You attract the energy that you put out. In some cases, people will not love you or treat you right because you sabotage situations with your own emotional poison when you don't believe that you deserve better.<br>2.Feel as if your partner's feelings are more important than yours. Therefore, you will stay in a relationship just because you don't want to hurt his feelings by leaving, even if you are not happy or don't share the same feelings anymore.<br>3.You may think you are selfish when you consider your own well-being when you think about leaving a relationship that does not make you happy, and so you choose to remain in a toxic relationship. | But the main reason is lack of self-love which causes you to accept living an unhappy life.<br>You put your health in last place and you exhaust your body with hard work<br>The result of that decision is that you are always sick, exhausted, and tired- physically and financially. Your energy is always low, you experience depression, and you feel you live a miserable life. |

We have a basic understanding of where self-love leads and the effects from the lack of it. Looking back now, I see myself like a skeleton walking through my life and using my body as a shell-just simply existing, feeling so insignificant, barely surviving, living in deep agony, and trapped in my own dark cage. I used to ask myself throughout the years why, as a child, I was forced to endure all the misery I was exposed to. The most amazing thing that self-love did for me was free me from the pain I lived in for so many years.

Yes! I can finally say that I'm pain free!

# CHAPTER 3

# Heal Your Pain through Belief and Self- Love

*"The only way to heal your internal pain, is by utilizing the power of positive thought."*
— Alina Balmos

Personally, I was not always a believer in God because I grew up in a religion that I could never understand and believe, and it never felt right for me. I always believed that there was a greater source out there, yet everyone called it something different; and that was all I knew about it.

Rather than call this source God, I prefer to refer to it as "The Source" or "The God of the Universe". I call it that because for me, it is the greatest power in the whole Universe. I truly believe that God/the Source is good and is pure love. This Source is in everyone and everything- including me and you! I will never forget someone who summed it up for me like this: "Imagine God being the ocean and you the drop of water"-and that was when I felt connected for the first time. I really felt on the inside that this is true, and this is what I personally believe.

I want you to believe in what makes you feel good, and what makes you feel whole because in the end, it is all about believing.

I do not ask you to believe the same, and it is not in my intention to do so. I read the Bible and I use everything that makes sense for me, which I find extremely helpful.

I personally believe that you don't need a religion to be connected with God. The relationship is just about belief. You need to believe and have faith in something…it's your choice in who or what. If you grow in love, in forgiveness, in peace, in kindness, and if you live in good and love without fear, God will be there for you.

I read a quote once in a wonderful book that states, "If you believe, nothing is impossible for you". Afterwards, I read it in the Bible also. Matthew 17:20 states, "If you have faith as small as a grain of mustard seed, nothing shall be impossible for you".

That made me want to believe more, and I started to affirm every morning and every night, three to five times per day, "I believe", and one day on my way to work, I prayed to the Universal God. I said, "God, here I am- doubting you, blaming you, and condemning you for so many years now. I'm ready, and I want to believe in you. As proof, I put my life, together with my family, in your hands. There is no harm in your hands, God. There is only benevolence. I know that whatever is going to happen will be what you think is best for me!"

Since that day, I never felt any serious stress and never experienced deep depressions because I know that I am in Good hands and somehow, I will find a way to get through it if I just believe!

I found an extremely helpful affirmation: "Everything is always working out for me!" I got this from my coach, Jenny. I used to repeat it every time I found myself in a stressful situation or when I was facing difficulties. It never really mattered how complicated the problem seemed to be because using the affirmation made me relaxed, calm, and sometimes, I could even deal with the problem with a big smile on my face. I knew I was in good hands!

For any problem, there is a solution. Believe that you have the power to pass through any struggles and any difficulties.

Here is a powerful affirmation that will help you solve all your problems: "Everything is always working out for me because I believe I am always divinely guided, and God has a solution to all my problems."

This train of thinking and speaking worked magic in my life!! Since I started to believe that I'm always divinely guided, and that God is always protecting me, my life has never been as hard as it used to be. When problems arose, and I couldn't see any solution, I put them in God's hands and it always worked out for me. When I felt fear, I asked God to stay by my side, and I felt relieved and empowered. When I felt too much pressure and my burdens became too heavy, I asked God to carry them for me.

When I felt lost and I didn't know what to do, I prayed for clarity.

I truly believe in the power of God and that there is a connection between your self-love and God. I couldn't connect with God until I learned to love and accept myself. No matter how much I tried to believe and pray, I felt as if my prayer was never answered.

I felt like as soon I entered in this world, I fell directly into a big dark hole, which I refer to as my own hell. That emotion was caused by the negative environment I grew up in during the most important years in my development as a child. That wasn't a good enough explanation for what caused that pain inside of me; and with time, I found that others were experiencing the same pain, but they never talked about it. So, I went back to the time when my pain left me and I tried to understand what changed and what I did to release the pain I was feeling.

The lessons I encountered after experiencing all these years of struggle and pain can be hard to accept or understand; however, I suggest viewing it as another way of seeing life.

Everyone wants to be happy, and everyone wants peace and fulfilment, right?

We all feel the need to experience those "emotions" because they are a part of us and a part of the source (God).

But what is happiness? And who is God?

Happiness it is a positive state… a part of what God represents. It comes from within yourself. It is a state of mind that comes from feelings like gratitude, peace, fulfilment, freedom, feeling present (not living in the past or in the future, being present in the moment mind body and spirit), being surrounded with abundance, forgiveness, etc. All those feelings which create happiness come from thoughts. There is no doubt about it! This has been scientifically proven time and time again.

This means that love, belief, and having faith in God must be also states of mind that come from your thoughts. After experiencing change in my life and growing my belief in God and myself love through affirmations, I came to the conclusion that there exists a connection between God and us, and it is affected by the power of our thoughts.

You can't be hating yourself or others for not accepting you for who you were created to be and still be able to personally relate to God. Why? Because God is goodness, ONLY good.

You can't be in a continuous negative state and relate to God

Therefore, everything revolves around love and happiness. Happiness can only be found through love, but it all begins in your mind. You connect with God through the power of thought.

God is everything that is good or positive, and everything that relates with this positive state relates to God. The source (God) can only be good and love, whereas everything that is related with a negative state is disconnected.

A few examples of words or feelings associated with the source God (everything Positive) include love, truth, life, peace, abundance, light, freedom, gratitude,
joy, fulfilment, forgiveness, happiness, laughter, blessings, powerful, energy, purpose, health, calm, believe, and patience.

Words and feelings associated with disconnection (everything negative) include pain, death, poverty, hate, agony, blame, depression, regret, darkness, negative, struggle, regret, sickness, ego, weakness, low self-esteem, powerless, lack of energy, anger, bad luck, feeling lost, and loneliness.

On a spiritual level, being disconnected from the Supreme Power (God) is the real reason for your pain, suffering, and depression. When you are disconnected, life is a real struggle. It is like living without a hand. You can still live but you will struggle, you will use more energy in every simple task, and you will feel useless, powerless, incomplete, and a burden for others. Just recently while working in a suicide awareness program, I found out that 90% of the suicidal attempts are caused by internal, emotional pain. All survivors declared that they never really wanted to die… they just wanted to get rid of the pain and that they are glad to be alive.

It took me a long time to understand this process. I finally found the answers and began to understand what causes inner pain and how to heal it!

One of my biggest discoveries was the fact we can control our thoughts. We are the only thinkers in our heads. Nobody can think for us, but if we do not have control over our thoughts, our thinking can be influenced by others. This led me to understand the hard reality that nobody can make you feel anything without you allowing it. In most cases, we allow almost everything to affect us in a non-deliberate way. Therefore, people or circumstances can affect you and your wellbeing only if you allow them to. Instead of reacting to a negative situation in your life, choose to respond with a non-judgmental attitude. Know that everyone is doing the best they can with the understanding and knowledge they have at that moment, and you shouldn't make the situation about the other person. Also keep in mind that you don't have to become a part of the problem or situation; it is ok to detach yourself from negative people and environments.

However, in my case was the lack of love for myself and the fact that I didn't know how to value myself or my needs, and C reflected what I lacked, which ultimately hurt me.

On top of that, my second big discovery was that your reality reflects what is inside of you.

My own emotional experiences were totally chaotic. I grew up in a victim state.

A victim state is a result of experiencing an increase of adrenaline which creates muscle tension, sudden shock, panic, and worry on a regular basis. All of this is produced by your brain and transmitted to your body. Therefore, when your brain is experiencing the victim state on a regular basis, it forms something I call victim cells.

Victim cells are neurons in your brain created from a set of negative, toxic beliefs which some people adopt at a young age or throughout life after experiencing an ongoing period in a victim state. This negative belief produces negative, destructive thoughts.

Once these beliefs reach the centre of our brain, these negative thoughts create a chemical substance called victim cells. That substance is then spread to the body, producing pain. Also, that chemical substance changes the flow of thought from positive to negative. Therefore, it breaks the connection with the source (God) and it can create different types of disease in our body like ulcers, diabetes, cancer, heart problems, hearing loss, etc. Once the victim cells are formed, they can only attract more of the same victim cells.

Therefore, a person with victim cells will experience depression, pain in the body, a constant pressure over their bodies, low energy, and they will constantly create and attract more negative situations or people, more problems, and everything seems to work against them. This cycle is repeated and until the flow of negative thoughts is broken. The person will constantly face difficulties, health problems, and bad luck will seem to follow them everywhere.

In analysing my own life, I conclude that I attracted more of what I already had inside of me. I attracted someone with the same victim cells and all kinds of stressful and painful situations. As a result, I continued to feed my spirit the same type of negativity that it thrived on for so many years. It is a tough process to break this addiction. You need to break the circle of negative thoughts and negative expectations in order to be successful.

I remember C and I used to break up every week and get ourselves to the point where our bodies could feel the panic and fear of losing one another. We did that by throwing damaging words and phrases such as, "I don't love you anymore", "I don't want you in my life", "I never loved you", and "I am in the relationship with you because I feel sorry for you." I clearly remember hurting C with those affirmations and I knew that what I was saying was not true, but I needed him to react so I could create the sensations that my body was asking for. C had exact same reaction.

In the first few days after we broke up, as soon after the phone stopped ringing, there was peace and quiet around me. I began to become agitated, and I felt like something was missing. Something didn't seem right. That feeling of calm and quite terrified me, and in addition to that was the fear of moving forward into something that seemed to be unknown. I had planned and imagined a life with him. We made plans for the future. We were together for so long that I was afraid of being alone without him. Because of that, I kept going back to give my body what it needed. When I was not with C or my parents anymore, I buried myself in work and I become a workaholic, working in a stressful environment. As you can clearly see in my story, I repeatedly faced hard times and no matter how far I moved or how different the environment and the society was, life was still a continuous struggle. I was constantly knocked down by life. Nothing changed until I changed. Nothing transformed until I understood that the problem was not the world around me, the problem was me. What was going on inside of me was the problem.

When I changed the way I looked at life, stopped acting and thinking as a victim, took control over my life, and accepted the responsibility for everything that happened in my life, everything changed. I went from everything happening against me to everything happening for me.

To prove this theory, I have my brothers that grew up with me in the same environment. They went through the same process, returned to the same unhealthy, toxic, and violent relationships, and continued to experience the same stress we experienced as young children. They are still fighting against this addiction in the present. I meet people in my life that had similar childhoods and faced similar continuous struggles as adults. It was proven to me time and time again that the victim cells are real and is one of the reasons why some of us face adversity on constant basis.

On a spiritual level, being disconnected from the Supreme Power (God) is the reason for our pain, suffering, and depression. When we are disconnected, life is a real struggle. It is like living without a hand. We can still live but will struggle, use more energy in simple tasks, and will feel useless, powerless, incomplete, and a burden.

When we are in the victim state, our flow of thought is negative. The way to connect with the source is the power of positive thought. An individual in a victim state breaks the connection with the source (God). I believe that when we are disconnected from the Source, we are not open to receiving anything from God. This is the reason why many individuals lose faith in God. To be connected, we need to accept ourselves first and be true with ourselves. Then, we need to be in a positive state of mind to make the way for God/the Source to connect through our love for ourselves.

That's why self-love and self-acceptance is the key to a balanced, happy, peaceful, and pain-free life.

To get out of the victim state and break the flow of negative thought, we need to reprogram our mind by using daily positive affirmations.

Affirmations are intentional. Affirmations force you to consciously choose your thoughts and words with the goal of eliminating negativity from your life and replacing it with something new and positive. An individual in a victim state must move from the negative to positive state of mind and use daily positive affirmations to grow in personal love and acceptance, eliminating all the negative feelings of the past and grow in belief in the Source, which is God.

Now here is the awesome news: you can control your thoughts and you can use the Mind Warder as the technique to assist you in doing that.

**The Methods and Techniques I Personally Used**

When I became mentally and physically exhausted at 19 years old, I made the decision to not allow my past or present decisions and condition to affect me.

That was when I discovered one of the wonderful abilities the mind holds, which I named The Mind Storage. Now we all know that we have the actual ability to store all our memories. You can store unwanted information such as traumatizing memories. This ability takes all of the unwanted information and stores it in a part of brain (in The Mind Storage) in a way that you are still aware of, but has no direct effect upon you anymore. You are not concentrating on that anymore! You do that by just refusing to think about the unwanted or unpleasant memories.

Since your thoughts determine your feelings, as soon as you don't have the negative thoughts as a focus anymore, your mood and the way you feel and view life changes. This is true! I experienced this and you can experience it, too. If you don't believe it, then test it right now!

Think for five minutes about something negative or something bad that happened to you; or just simply imagine a very negative scenario, and notice how you feel! Then, switch your thoughts to a positive and wonderful memory. Think about the happiest day of your life for another five minutes and notice the change in the way you feel, and most importantly, acknowledge the fact that you can control your thoughts and your mood!!!

I discovered this ability when I decided I didn't want to think about those memories anymore; soon after, I realized I haven't felt the same. At the time, I didn't know what had happened, but afterwards, I began to use this ability consistently in my life. I started to concentrate on finding solutions instead of focusing on the problem.

I divided the Mind Storage into two parts: one that stores all the good memories, which I called "Treasure Box", and one that stores all the bad memories of the past that affect our present and all negative thoughts, which I called the "Wastage Box".

I used this technique as a coping mechanism mostly for the moment when the pain was too unbearable, and you feel you can't deal with it anymore. It gives you relief, somehow making space in your mind for other thoughts and keeps you functioning at another level. How fascinating and powerful is that!!

I also used it to break the cycle of negative thinking and to free myself of the victim state by refusing to think about painful memories or having negative thoughts. When the negative thoughts came to my mind, I would visualise my Mind Warder using his sword and eliminating them. I know it sounds hard to understand. It is mostly about acknowledging the ability of the wastage box and the rest comes naturally. I was full of unwanted memories which had a long-term effect on me and my brothers. Both of my brothers said they had anger problems, constant fatigue, and panic attacks. It is important to deal with traumatizing memories which have a huge impact on your life.

I wrote about my painful memories many times in detail, without knowing why I was doing it. I began keeping journals and wrote about my feelings from age 8 or 9, a very short time after I learned how to write. I used to stay outside at night and share my feelings and pain as I talked to the moon. I even sung all my pain to the moon. I didn't know why I was doing it. Nobody told me to do it, but I just did it because it made me feel so good doing it. Those methods worked like therapy for me by providing me with an outlet to release all the pain, the hate, and the destructive poison that came from those memories and hard moments that I held inside of me. I also practiced forgiveness and letting go of the hate I felt for people that hurt me. Just recently, I started to do some more internal work to heal the wounds I was not able to heal myself. There are some things in life that you just can't do alone! Writing about my feelings helped me to make peace with my past and it helped me to see all the pain and struggle as a blessing. In other words, I made the decision to change the way I saw my past up until that point. What I did was create a shift in my thinking- that's the ability we all have. Some call it the observer, or the watcher- I call it the Mind Warder!

You can't use a power that you don't know that you have! It's like having two legs, but never actually understanding the purpose of your legs, never learning how to walk, and never figuring it out…just crawling for the rest of your life- as simple as that! You need to acknowledge it and be aware of it so you can use that power.

However, most people don't take time to acknowledge what is in their minds; they don't know what they are capable of, which leads to a person feeling powerless and out of control. Information is truly a gold mine. Think about it: every day you are using your abilities, and your mind never stops functioning. However, the less you know about your abilities and powers, the smaller your expectations are. That means that you are using your abilities based on how much you think you can accomplish. The more limited you are in your thinking, the less you use your capacities.

From the moment I understood how the mind works, one of the best things I ever did for myself was to eliminate TV, radio, and newspaper from my life. Today I carefully choose what I feed my mind, what type of music I listen to, and what type of movies I watch. I personally replace all the toxic "tools of manipulation" with my passion in researching and learning more about my mind and my ability as an individual. I believe that everything I need to know will be revealed to me at the right time. I'm not afraid of missing any important information. I never missed one in 3 years.

We are controlled by TV, radio, newspaper, by our negative friends or even family's negative believes. If we don't take control over our thoughts we are controlled by everything around us and we react to everything. We just go with the flow through life, having no control and we go along with the flow, with no direction, like a ship without a captain. What do you think is going to happen with it? It is probably going to sink somewhere because it is just floating aimlessly, hitting whatever it comes across. And eventually, the damages will sink the ship. Take the lead. Be the captain of your own ship!!! If you don't, my friend, then you condemn yourself to an unhappy, unfulfilled life, blaming life for your struggles and feeling powerless.

In accordance with all the techniques already mentioned above, I used affirmations to grow my self-love and my belief (chapter 2).

Remember, everything starts with a thought. "I believe" is a thought that needs to be planted in the garden of your mind. Always repeat, "I believe everything is possible for me!" Memorize it until it is a part of you, and the rest will flow naturally!

Changing your beliefs and thoughts about yourself, improving, making progress, and moving to another level in life is like a hard, long winter. You will encounter stress, disappointments, hard work, and loads of days with zero results. But you know what? Winter never lasts forever! When winter is gone, the land is ready-and so will you be ready if you just survive the winter. Winters are created to prepare you! All you must do is survive the difficult moments and your achievement will be waiting for you at the end!

Now, you know that winter will come every year, and some winters will hit you harder than others. When you are ready to quit, ready to give up, and when you really think you have no power to keep going, just close your eyes and tap into that seed of deep determination. That's it! No matter what you do, do not stop, and do not give up!

Say to yourself, "I can do this! I will make it to the end! I will never give up because giving up is not an option for me! I haven't survived all those past winters, and I didn't endure all the pain and tears to stop now and just give up! I need to get my reward for surviving the agony!"

Change what you think about yourself, and everything will change for you! |

However, it took me three long years to transform my life and learn to resist the need for drama by using all the principles and techniques written in this book. With patience, consistency, reprogramming my mind with daily positive affirmations and healthy thoughts, using the power of the Mind Warder and Wastage box techniques (refusing to think negative thoughts) in addition to the power of self-love and my belief in the Source (God), I finally found my peace and I succeeded in defeating the addiction.

Always remember that the key to connect with God and find peace within yourself lies in self-acceptance, self-love, and the power of positive thinking.

Here is a little plan to follow so you can heal your pain:

1. Create a daily morning ritual where you listen or read selflove affirmations out loud for at least 30 minutes every morning (you can find some examples of mine written in chapter two). You can also use YouTube as a source.
2. Use the Mind Warder technique throughout the day to maintain control of your thoughts. Also use positive quotes to help you stay focused on positivity throughout the rest of the day and pay attention to the words you use about yourself.
3. Grow your belief in the source, affirming "I believe!" every morning in the first 5 minutes you wake up and as many times as you can throughout the day. If you are already a believer in God, focus on self-love, self-acceptance, and positive affirmations.

4. Be conscious of what you expose your mind to. Try to eliminate the negative news on television, radio, and newspapers.
5. Find a support group of positive people that will support you throughout this journey.
6. Whatever do, don't stop until you see change in your life. It is ok if you miss a day or a week; the secret is to persevere through the difficult times and don't give up trying. The results are guaranteed!
7. Remember that change is a life time commitment. You always must be in control, so never let go of the Mind Warder technique.

# CHAPTER 4

# The Power of Choice and Decision The Greatest Abilities We Possess

*"If you see struggles as obstacles, they will become your obstacles. Look at your struggles as blessings and let them lift you up."*

—Alina Balmos

There was once a young man that just finished high school, and he felt ready to go face the world and accomplish something in his life. God brought him to a 3-way crossroad and told him to choose the direction he wanted to go. The boy looked to his right, and he saw a narrow, damaged, and steep road which was full of obstacles and very difficult to walk through. At the end of that road lie his dreams, his deepest desires, and his true happiness, but it looked so far away that it seemed impossible for him to ever reach that. He looked to the path on his left and noticed that it was an easy road, easy obstacles, with a normal, everyday average life -a life where you do what you think it is normal to do, what others told you is best to do, and not what you truly love and desire. Then, he looked at the road that lie straight in front of him. Three meters away from him was a huge box filled with money. He said to himself, "Why take right or left when I have everything I need in front of me, and with this I can create the life I want!"

He went straight to the money and as soon he grabbed the money, he fell into a big hole where he lived in fear and pain for five years. He prayed to God and asked him for another chance, promising to God that he would make the right decision this time!

God listened to his prayer and put him again at the same 3-road crossing. This time, the boy was determined to make the right decision. He looked again to his right, and said to himself "I can't let myself be fooled again. It seems impossible to attain true happiness and be truly rich in every area of my life. I have one chance, and I can't blow it again to take a chance on the road to the right. I must be realistic and make the right decision!"

He then said "Ok God, I'm ready!" He went on the left road where he spent his life having a job and raising three children together with his loving wife, but he never could feel accomplished. There was an emptiness inside that felt like an eternal void. Every night, he went to sleep with the regret of never taking a chance with the road on the right, and at age 45 he got sick. Right before he died, he prayed one more time to God:

"God, you gave me a mission. You have given me options and abilities to choose and make decisions. You blessed me with all the powers and abilities I needed to fulfil that mission, and I failed in accomplishing it! I never believed that it was possible for me, so I never tried. I finally understand, God...every morning you put me on the same crossing, and until my last breath, every morning you gave me the chance to go on the right road. I never took it God because I didn't believe it was possible. I never truly believed in me. Therefore, I never believed in you God, and that you would protect me and guide me all the way on the right!

Please forgive me, God!" We waste our time living unaccomplished lives and barely daring to dream about big things because we are so afraid of being disappointed, so we do not allow ourselves to dream too big or have big expectations. Somehow, we got this idea that accomplishing our dreams is not possible. I grew up with this idea that it was bad to dream big because people would call you a dreamer, and then laugh and say you are crazy. They would say, "Look at that girl. She thinks she is going to be famous one day. She lives so far away from reality, the poor girl! She is crazy if she thinks she will get further than the next town!" These types of people also believe that it is impossible to have everything in life. They sound like it is selfish to want to have a happy family, a job that you love doing, and to be healthy and wealthy!

How crazy is it not to dream, to not have big expectations for ourselves, and walk around full of mediocrity, just accepting things that come our way and settling for the very least. Believe me, as absurd as it sounds, it's exactly like having two legs but spending all your life struggling to move, all because you don't know the purpose of your legs and we don't believe that is possible for us to walk.

This situation is exactly what some of us do every day with our power and our dreams. We can accept the "reality" or keep trying to walk until we finally stand up on our own and make the impossible possible.

No other living creature on earth has the ability to consciously think and make decisions, make choices, and have the power to control their thoughts and their lives. Every moment is a decision to wake up and eat healthy, to start working out, to go on a different street, and decide to say a nice thing to someone or call someone. From the moment you wake up until you go back to sleep, you make decisions that will determine your tomorrow. I know I probably repeat this many times throughout this chapter, but looking around me, I see that our ability to make decisions is taken for granted when in fact, it is the greatest asset we possess.

We have all the ability to get all the skills we need. It was scientifically proven that we can develop a lot of the skills we need to accomplish almost anything we want in life.

Look at my story. I was considered a dummy and I was very slow in accomplishing tasks in learning. I always took my time, and sometimes I would need 30 minutes to wash dishes, or half of a day to clean my room; I was just moving slow and I was criticized by my parents a lot because of it. That really hurt me because I remember that every time I was cleaning or washing dishes, my only thoughts were "I'm going to clean better than anyone else, and I won't miss a spot." My intentions were always to do the best work and to check all the details. I never thought about the time it took for me to complete a task because I was thinking about the quality of my work at that time; however, everyone else seemed to be concerned about how long it would take me to finish something. I couldn't understand why they were so bothered.

Instead of communicating their desires for me to be more timely, all I heard was that it was wrong to be slow and that I needed to have more speed, or else I would have problems keeping a job in my adulthood because nobody wants to keep a slow worker.

You see, I didn't think it was possible to move fast and simultaneously do a quality job, and the only reason that I felt that way was because no one told me it was possible! It was as simple as that. I never heard the magical words, "Alina, you can do it!" Communication and encouragement for completion of simple tasks is important for young children. I always had to put in twice as much effort than everybody else just to stay at the same level with the rest. I seemed to have problems remembering things I said or I did. For example, if you would ask me to remember a number for a certain period, I would struggle and panic that I would forget it. I used to try so hard to keep that number in my head, but I couldn't because instead of focusing on the number, I concentrated on the fear of forgetting the number instead of remembering.

You see, we can't focus on two different things at the same time. The strongest thoughts, the thoughts we choose to focus our energy on, will always win. It is just the way it works. My self-defeating beliefs limited my ability to accomplish anything, which I then expressed through my actions. These actions were demonstrated by my inability to excel in school and complete simple tasks.

My parents couldn't rely on me to accomplish any tasks and therefore, they didn't seem to have too many expectations from me or for my future. I remember when I was in school, I was always simply present and I never wanted to be involved in anything because I didn't want to make a fool out of myself. I already knew that I couldn't do anything well, so therefore, I didn't even try. Every day in school, I was praying to not be seen or asked anything by the teacher. As a result, I had no progress. Every day I was just hoping to make it to the end of that day without being seen. When I was about 12 years old, I couldn't read the time. I was falling more and more behind everyone, which was evidence that I was useless and dumb. I saw all my colleagues progressing, getting smarter, going to the universities, but there I was at 17 years old, working in a kebab shop making sandwiches 12 hours a day, five days a week. I was frying chicken and working 8 to 9 hours in 60 -70 degrees with no break, and not even a drop of water. I used to wonder why everyone I grew up with was doing so well. We grew up together and were exposed to the same information. I wondered what made them so different. My only explanation at that time was that they haven't been through what I'd been through, and they had money, but I didn't. They were lucky and my life was full of bad luck. I was moaning and complaining every day. I would say my miserable story to everyone that was willing to listen. I hated my job with all my heart. I cried so many mornings on my way to work, but each time I went to work, I had given my best and I challenged myself to move fast and do a quality job. In 7 months, I developed my skills as a fast, effective worker, but because it was so hard for me to find a job and this job was my first, I didn't think I could do better than that. I stayed in that job, dreaming every day of working as a waitress and being clean, having beautiful coloured nails, and nice perfume. I stayed in that job until I terrorised all my colleagues with my negativity and I was eventually fired. However, I was blessed to find a job as a waitress two days later.

Even in that job, I was miserable and treated like a dummy because that was what I believed about myself. You reflect externally what you feel internally, and based on my beliefs, this was the reality I created for myself. People saw me the way I saw myself and treated me accordingly.

Nothing changed until the night that I failed to make a change in my family, and my father hit me after I asked him to quit drinking. All that night, I cried and bounced like a lunatic swaying forward and backwards, sitting in my bed, punching myself in the chest with my fists because I couldn't stand the pain anymore. I repeated that I would make sure he would be sorry for what he did, and I will show everyone who I am!

Do you understand why that was an important for me?

It was important because I changed the way I saw my situation, and I made the shift in my thinking. That, dear friend, is the secret of change!

I stopped viewing my situation and my past a reason why I couldn't be successful, and I stopped accepting a role as a victim. In that moment, I began to use all the pain and struggles to work in my favour, and I began to free myself from the bondage! I became stubborn in proving them wrong.

I used to say to myself repeatedly, "I'm going to prove everyone wrong! I'm not stupid, retarded, or useless! I'm committed to make something of myself and do something with my life. I will make sure that one day, all of my family will apologize to me for not believing in me, for putting me down, and for not understanding me."

That simple change in thinking from, "This is who I am, this is my life, and they are right…I'm a loser and there is no point for me to even try to be better. I just need to swallow my suffering" to "I will show you who I am. I will make sure you will regret all of those awful statements, and I will prove to everyone the contrary," completely changed my trajectory. I used my stubbornness in my favour and as a motivating tool to improve my train of thinking and my life.

Wayne Dyer said, "When you change the way you look at things, the things you look at change." This is as true as knowing that you need air to survive!!!

With the power of will, determination, and practice, I worked my way up to being the author I am today.

My story proves that our decisions dictate our quality of life and future. When I decided that it was time to stop being a victim and take responsibility over my life, my days and my future changed. God gave us this gift of creation, which is the possibility to turn our lives around and be the best version of ourselves. He gives us this opportunity at the beginning of each day, but some of us live our whole lives never using that blessing and never really giving ourselves a chance to be truly happy and fulfilled, because somehow, we do not believe it is possible. And we live, just to die full of regret!

The most important thing that we all need to be aware of is that we were not born slow, stupid, angry, selfish, or any other negative thing. We can be who we want to be and we can do what we want to do. God, the Source, gave us all the power we need.

Practice is the key to everything. If we are slow, we can become fast by practicing, and if we struggle in learning, it doesn't mean we are stupid. It means we haven't learned how to learn, and we need to ask someone to show us how to do it and discover what works best for us. For example, I learn faster by listening. My mother used to learn faster by writing everything down, while others associate words with things that are easy for them to remember.

We were all born with the ability to learn, but we have to develop it in a similar way that toddlers learn how to walk. We have the legs, but we have to learn how to walk first and walking is something you develop with practice. The more you practice, the easier it becomes for you to learn. And believe me, there's no rush. Life is not a competition, but people make it that way. It is not about who learns first or who gets rich and successful first.

For me, life is all about progress, becoming the best version of myself, and enjoying the ride. What I came to discover later was that we come to this world with a purpose hidden inside of us. For many of us, nobody ever told us that we are special and that we are here on earth with a purpose. Therefore, I didn't know who I was or what I was meant to do, and I felt lost for many years. The state of being lost and not knowing what you want or do with your life comes from the internal confusion from not knowing who you truly are. Our purpose doesn't come with instructions attached. It simply is a part of us, of who we were born to be. We all are powerful. We are miracles, and we have the power to choose and to create the life we want to live. We were born to be great and happy, to experience life, and fulfil our purpose and our life mission. We are all a tiny part of the

Source, God. I believe that the desires we have for happiness, love, and fulfilment are different for everybody and that we are all unique when we allow ourselves to be who we truly are. Then, we find our purpose in life.

We should never settle with what we think is normal or with what others are telling us is normal. Instead, look inside of yourself and ask, "What is it that I desire but feel that I'm never going to get? Do I truly feel that it is impossible? What thoughts make me feel good?" The answers are going to guide you in the right direction.

The secret of my change comes from a simple shift in thinking. Deciding to stop being a victim, deciding to stop letting my past affect my future, choosing to invest in myself, and believing that it is possible for me to learn and improve are habits that changed my life. Everyone can learn if they just learn how to learn. Gaining knowledge was also an inspiration behind my transformation and development. Each and every time, my willingness to learn new information and incorporate change was the key to helping me catapult my life and spirit.

I learned from my childhood that you can only lead by example, and that we are our child's first and primary example as to how they should live and respond to situations. Children copy our reactions and our attitudes, and they pay more attention to what we do than what we say.

Children always need to be reassured of their amazing possibilities, that they can do whatever they put their mind to, and that they are strong and beautiful. This is how they form a strong foundation of self-confidence and self-love. When they go and face the world- in school or kindergarten- and encounter people who say they are ugly, stupid, and other mean names, they will be ready and they will not believe those words. They will come to us to reassure them that those things are not true. And they will grow up with strong, confident personalities.

From my perspective, nobody is to blame for the way I grew up, or for the lack of information or communication. I love, respect, and appreciate my parents with all my heart because I know they did the best they could with the knowledge and understanding that they had as a young, inexperienced couple. All that they learned from their parents was ignorance, poverty, violence, and lack of communication which they perpetuated in their own adulthood within their family.

I was affected at the beginning by my environment at home and I internalized all that I was hearing about myself; and I believed everything without a doubt. But as I grew up, I liked to challenge myself. Therefore, if someone told me that I couldn't do something, I would go and do it no matter how foolish it was. But somehow when a thought would pop up in my head and say, "Alina you can't do that!" I would listen and not act. It's interesting how we react when others discourage us and tell us we can't do something and how we take it so easy from when it's coming from within ourselves.

In my opinion, the only thing that stops us from following our dreams or making a huge progress is our mind. For example, my biggest dream as a child was to serve in the Army, but I was rejected because I couldn't afford to pay my way into the Academy. So, I decided to enrol in high school sports, stay physically ready, and try again after four years. But to get into the high school, I had to be evaluated and pass the test first in order to be accepted.

I was so disappointed and filled with anger and hate towards people. Everybody seemed to want money in exchange for an opportunity. The teacher that was supposed to prepare me for the assessment totally ignored me because I hadn't given him any money. So in the middle of the assessment, I said to myself "There's no point in running. They will fail me anyway," and so I stopped. I quit in the middle of the assessment and because of that, I was not accepted into the high school sports! My aunt ran to me and slapped me on the face in front of a full stadium of people for giving up. I felt extremely embarrassed. I cried and I ran away.

But guess what? I never lived with the embarrassment. I lived instead with the regret.

I let my mind discourage me, and you know what? All I had to do was run to the end and I would had been accepted. The exam was not about who finished first; it was about getting the miles done. If I wouldn't have listened to my mind, I would've passed the exam. The idea that I couldn't do it was just in my head.

The lesson that I learned from this experience is that embarrassment never lasts forever, but the regret does! Never let your mind discourage you and tell you that you can't achieve your goal. If you have a dream, go for it with everything in you, regardless of the embarrassment, fear, rejection, or disappointment. Those experiences are temporary! If you decide to give up, you will live with the regret for the rest of your life!

Sometimes it is important to doubt our thoughts or the information we receive. Imagine your mind like a car, and you are the driver. Now from day one, you were told that the car goes just 40 miles an hour. All we know is what we've been told, and so we believe it.

If we just believe what we are told and never doubt it (like I did for a few years believing I was retarded and that I had a slow mind), we will travel all our life at only 40 miles an hour, never knowing our car's true capacity!

As the driver, you need to know your car's capacity. You need to try and test it to see if that is all the power that car has, and if what you have been told is true. Always be curious… that's the only way you can find out the truth. Test your powers and your own capacities and you will be surprised what you can do just by believing you can!

Doubt your thoughts by asking the questions, "Is what I'm thinking true? I really can't do that? How will I ever know if I never try? Is this all I can do, or is there more in me? How would I know if I never challenge myself?"

Remember that just because you don't know about something doesn't mean it doesn't exist or is not possible- be open and do not limit yourself. Explore and ask.

Be curious. Don't travel all your life at only 40 miles per hour!

Look at it from this perspective: you've already done the things that everyone else has done and their strategies haven't gotten you too far. Maybe it is time to take the right road and to view life from a different perspective. Everything starts with your mind. The subconscious mind is the greatest power a human possesses! You hold the power of decision and the power to choose what you are focusing on. Therefore, the solution to overcome a negative situation usually lies in the way we look at the situation.

In other words, the way you look at life or think about life can have a massive influence in your life. If you have negative thoughts about life, you will encounter negative experiences. However, if you have positive thoughts you will encounter positive happy situations.

Along with my own experience, and through my studying and researching, here are some other ways of seeing life.

# 10 WAYS TO CHANGE THE TRAJECTORY OF YOUR LIFE

## 1. LOOK AT THINGS FOR WHAT THEY ARE

**Live with a non-judgmental attitude.**

When we first see someone or something that is unfamiliar or different than what we are used to, it seems natural that our mind immediately starts to judge, almost as if we are programmed to do it. And we immediately have thoughts like, "Look at that! How ugly! How stupid is this? I don't like him. Why is he / she like that?" etc. Because of that, we should always look twice at everything. The second view is when you look again, at the same situation from a different perspective. You have to be sure that you look at everything for what it IS and not what it represents.

Growing up in a village, we had all sorts of animals. Some of the animals were my friends. One day, a tiny baby chicken hatched and wasn't able to use his legs. My father saw no use for him and wanted to throw it away, but I asked him to let me do it. The plan, as crude as it was, was for me to throw it away in a big mountain of trash. I held it in my hand, but I couldn't do it; I saw a tiny baby like me. A living soul. Instead, I hid it in a secret place and I fed it every day. I played with him, and I shared my feelings with him. He became my best friend. I massaged his tiny legs and I practiced waking with him. Six months later as I was coming from school, I saw my chicken walking on his own feet! I felt so happy and proud of my miracle! I walked away from this experience with a big lesson: everyone deserves a chance to live and fulfill their purpose. Everyone and everything has a purpose…even a creature as minute as my chicken, whose purpose was to give me a lesson.

I believe behind every gesture and behaviour lies a pure soul that has a story. Nobody wants to be a certain way. Due to our own ignorance, in many cases, life transforms us in several ways. We become selfish, mean, and disrespectful towards others etc., so do not take anything personal. Everyone is doing the best they can with the understanding they have at that moment. Everyone has a purpose and the right to a chance to fulfill their purpose.

To have harmony and peace in our lives, we have to stop looking for things to blame, people to judge and criticise. Instead, look for good in everything and more good will come to us.

## 2. LIVE WITH A NEVER GIVE UP ATTITUDE

**The baby with a never give up attitude is still in you!**

When you were born, were you born with strong muscles, ready to walk, talk, run and play? Of course not, it takes a while until you are strong enough to just sit down straight without collapsing isn't it?

You tried and tried to stand and walk until you learned how to walk. Giving up was not an option.

The only thing that got me out of every struggle was my never giving up attitude. No matter the situation, I kept on going forward. I challenged life until life let me be. I survived the storm. I really believe that the secret in any success or achievement lies in a never giving up attitude.

I think we all are going to be tested by life, and only the ones that survive the winters are going to meet the real success in life. We have to keep getting up no matter how many times we are knocked down and knock at the door of freedom until it is going to open for us.

I promise you that it will open eventually, and you will get out of the storm.

## 3. SEE STRUGGLES AS BLESSINGS

**Live always looking for the positive side of every struggle.**

I heard a story once which said that when God created the birds, he first created them without wings. One day, God asked the birds, "It is anyone here that wants to try some burdens? All the birds answered -No, no thank you!

But God convinced two or three eventually, and then the birds asked God, "Where do you want us to carry it?" And God responded, "You will carry it on your back!"

So, then God put 2 beautiful wings on each bird's back.

The other birds asked them, "Why on earth would you want to carry those wings too? It is not enough that you must carry your fathers every day?"

The other birds said: "Look!" And they begin to fly

Our challenges are nothing else than God's wings on our back that will get us close to ourselves, to our goals, and close to God. Every challenge that God gives us is nothing more than two wings on our back that will grow beautifully. God knows why everything is happening, and He's never wrong. Always remember that God grows our wings painfully, but He has a purpose for all our struggles! So be grateful for your struggles.

## 4. BELIEVE THAT YOU ARE ALWAYS DIVINELY GUIDED

**If are open to receive, your prayers will always be answered.**

When we believe that we are in good hands and that everything is always working out for us no matter the problem, our life becomes more beautiful, more peaceful, and stress free.

Nothing gives us more relief than a strong faith,

Put your life in the Source's hand, and always stay in a positive flow of thought so God can hold you and support you!

## 5. LIFE IS NOT ABOUT WHAT WE GET, IT IS ABOUT WHAT WE BECOME IN THE PROCESS

**The key to your own freedom, lies in your mind not in your bank account.**

Money and all the material things are important, but we should never make them apart of who we are. We are already enough. When you get to the core of a person, and when you become full of forgiveness, full of peace, and full over love, you don't need much because you are already happy. Isn't that what we all want?

We like to over complicate life, but think about it. At the end of life, nobody ever died saying, "I'm happy. I was rich in this life, but most of people die saying that they haven't lived enough!

Life is about what you become in the process, and the key to your own freedom, lies in your mind and not in your bank account.

## 6. AS LONG AS YOU LIVE, YOU ARE A WORK IN PROGRESS.

"Suffering is Caused by Ignorance"- Dalai Lama

Knowledge is the inspiration behind my transformation and development. My willingness to learn new information and incorporate change was the key that helped me catapult my life and spirit. I strongly believe that, this pattern of continually going back to the source of your suffering is caused by ignorance. Please note that ignorance does not mean "stupid", as it is often incorrectly used. Ignorance simply means a lack of knowledge or understanding. The key to end the cycle of suffering caused by ignorance is to realize that you have the power to end your suffering. You have the power to take control of your life, and end your suffering. The key to this is to examine your life, and find out what is causing suffering in your life, and to actively seek to eliminate those causes of suffering, no matter how painful the elimination process may be.

## 7. LOVE YOURSELF LIKE A MOTHER LOVES HER CHILD- UNCONDITIONALLY

**We are miracles of the universe and we were born to be great!**

When you love yourself in a pure and honest way in the same fashion that a mother loves her child, I guarantee that you will become unstoppable and you will achieve your goals with no doubt. You will never feel lost again, and you will not feel the need to look for reasons to stay motivated and keep pushing through the difficult times because YOU will be an enough reason. You will no longer need to depend on someone to serve as an accountability partner because you became serious about holding yourself accountable, and you will wake up ready to serve and care for yourself. You will wake up because you will know that your life and your body is your responsibility. You have to live with yourself for the rest of your life.

You can hide from people if you try, but you can never hide from your own self and your own regrets.

You can either go to sleep and wake up with remorse, or wake up and go through what is necessary to gain your peace, your happiness, and your fulfilment! Why not cross the finish line of life with a big smile on your face while saying, "I did everything I could for myself and for others!"

## 8. THE MIND WARDER IS YOUR ABILITY TO CONTROL YOUR LIFE AND MIND.

Everyone can change. For any change desired, the only thing that needs changing is your perspective!!

Everything starts in your mind, and the Mind Warder is the power within you. it is a tool if you like or a technique you can use to change your beliefs and your perspectives., Please acknowledge it and start to create your own life.

## 9. WRITE DOWN WHAT YOU WANT

Write down what you want in detail and make it reality.

I'm telling you, all you have to do (apart from taking action) is write things down. There is a power in writing things down that works like magic; it makes everything so clear for you. It brings clarity and allows you to realize who you are, who you want to be, where you are now, and where you want to be which immediately helps you realize the steps that you need to take to accomplish your goals.

Now, I met people that were laughing and who would say things such as, "I'm not writing anything down. Where do you think I am, in school? Give me a break!"

I don't hang around those types people anymore, that's for sure. But I have a question: Do you think you, your life, and the people you care about deserve the best version of you? Are you willing to give 30 minutes of your time to write your goals and your dreams down? Do you think that you and your future deserve that big of a hustle?

I think you do and so should you!

## 10. MAKE A DECISION TO TRULY CHANGE

**Behind any change, goal or achievement we desire to achieve, is the feeling of happiness that we are after.**

Make the decision within yourself to change instead of just merely stating that you want to change. Attach the decision to a feeling. Behind any change, goal, or achievement we desire to accomplish is the feeling that we are after. We all want to feel happy, fulfilled, and accomplished, don't we?

If you want to make a change now in your life, a great way to start is by breaking a bad habit or change the way you see yourself. You can start by answering the following questions: Why you want to change? How would that change impact your life and how would you feel when you achieve the desire change? What do you need to do to achieve the feelings that come with the change? As soon you find out the answers to these questions, write them down and start to create small goals that will lead you to see the change you are after.

As we arrive to the end of our journey, I hope that I answered some of your questions and helped you gain a better understanding about what may be going on inside of yourself. I have exposed my whole life experience so I can clearly point out the changing points in my life to serve as a clear example on how changing your perspective can impact your life, and what kind of thinking leads to a happy, peaceful, emotional, pain-free existence.

I want to end by sharing my intention for this book. I hope that this book will help you view life in a different way...a way that will bring happiness, joy, and fulfilment in your life . Let this book help you release the pain and create peace inside of you. Let your faith grow as a light in every cell of your body and reunite you once again and forever with the source God.

P.S.

If by any chance you ask yourself, what happened with my victim cells? I say they died of starvation.